WHERE'S HOME?

W.A.M. MacKenzie

D1579276

www.wammackenzie.co.uk

BrightSpark

www.selfpublishforfree.co.uk

DEDICATION

'In memory of Peter - the boy who walked on water.'

W.A.M. MacKenzie is the author of three novels
available on Kindle via Amazon.co.uk:
'Bitter Fruit'
'Doxie'
and
'The Obedient Servant'

www.wammackenzie.co.uk

Prologue.

When a sheep is being shorn the shearer's aim to get the fleece off in a single sheet so that when it is turned over it lies like a creamy cloud.

Would that memory came away in a single sheet. That I could shear my sheep and lay the fleece before you, whole and in order.

Sadly though, no pure fleece this!

More like the random gatherings of wool picked off the barbs of fences or from the whin bushes. No order, no sequence. No certainty even from what year the wool comes and certainly no idea, which was the donor sheep.

Do I remember?

Or did I dream?

Or was I told about it and took it to myself?

Forgive me, for I do not know.

PRONCY

If you are ever up that way, travelling north with Dornoch nestled down beside its firth to your right, cast your eyes left and on the hill is Proncy. The farmhouse stands out in front of a little belt of trees and behind the trees are the two farm cottages and the big steading.

A few years back if you had looked down on these farm cottages you would have seen – between the cottage fronts and their small gardens – a pathway of pebbles. And with a little wooden wheel barrow and the coal shovel a small, chubby child in shorts, knitted jersey, wool stockings and tough black boots would be seen busily filling his barrow with pebbles and transporting them to add to his pile at the other end of the path. Oddly he sported a small cap of the schoolboy variety. He had insisted that he wanted a bonnet like Granddad's but his mother could not find a bonnet in his size so got him a cap instead and came home and convinced me with the shameful help of Jeannie and Granddad that it was indeed a bonnet.

Yes, of course, the chubby child was me.

"Here, Willie." Mum was interrupting the worker. "This is Granddad's piece, he's forgotten it. Take it round, he's in the thrashing shed."

She proffered me a square metal box. It had started life as a container for sheep medicine capsules but was such a perfect size for a Piece Box that Josie the shepherd had passed them out all over the place.

"There's a wee bit sandwich in there for you too," Mum said.

At the time I was gullible enough to believe that a cap was a bonnet so I swallowed the lie that Granddad had forgotten his piece with no trouble at all. Now I know it was a trick to make me feel useful and grown up and also, as a bonus, gave me the treat of lunching in the thrashing shed with Granddad.

Off I set, round the end of the house and then along by the open sided sheds where there were carts and piles of harrows and all sorts of tackle thrust in the semi dry to await its season. Each bit of machinery was white with guano for the hens perched in there, on the rafters and on the machines. And practically every rafter joint was host to a mud nest of swallow or swift and they shot in and out like demented darts.

At the end of the cart shed there was a left turn past the dung heap and the now resting waterwheel and in the half door. Thankfully the sneck was off, I would never reach over. I was expected.

Granddad and Calder sat in the straw in the high gloomy shed. Above and behind them there was a loft, the floor of which stopped in a precipice face. Above the cliff was hay, below was deep in straw. It was later that the arrangement bore in on me as a great place for leaping into space and plunging into great billows of sweet smelling straw.

"Here, boy!" Granddad patted down the wee space of straw between himself and Calder. "I was just looking for my tin."

"There's a slice in there for me," I said as I jiggled into the space between their elbows.

"Only right that the messenger gets his piece," Calder said.

Calder was a small stout man who came from Birichen for some part time jobs on Proncy. He, of course, had a bonnet and a moustache but his moustache was no match for Granddad's. Granddad was known as "Big Kenny" but he was not big – he was tall, tall and thin with a long, lean face and a beaked nose and beneath it a moustache which sloped down at the ends of his mouth to give him a soulful look, an impression which was a lie if ever there was one.

"Here," Granddad poured his milky tea from the flask into the flask top and passed it to me. "Give it a blow first."

It did not occur to me that it was strange that he should remember his flask but forget his piece box. His flask was fragile and valuable so could not safely be entrusted to my dubious care.

"What's on yer piece the day, Kenny?" Calder asked.

"Butter and crowdy", Granddad replied.

"Man, I have a nice bit of ham the day – off the bone if I'm not mistaken," Calder smacked his lips.

"He has not, Granddad," I was appalled by such lies - I could see into his piece box, "He has jam."

"Aye, but it's Ham jam," said Calder.

"It's not," I cried. "It's rasp."

"And I have two chocolate biscuits," Calder ignored my protest.

This required checking out. Chocolate biscuits were not often seen and when I peered into his box, yes there were two biscuits, but there was certainly no chocolate.

"They're just plain," I protested.

"Ginger snaps by the look of them," Granddad chuckled.

"See," I turned crossly to Calder. "They're not chocolate biscuits."

"Not now," Calder nodded and laughed, "No, they're not chocolate now - but they were this morning. I licked the chocolate off at half-yoking."

That did not ring true to me but I just ate my piece, thick with last night's butter and crowdy.

"Are you finished your piece?" Calder asked me.

"Yes," I said shortly.

"Will you have one of my biscuits?"

"No," I yelped.

"No, what?" Granddad prompted gently.

"No, I won't have one of the biscuits he's been licking," I corrected myself primly and they both, for some unknown reason, laughed.

In the afternoon I resumed my business with the barrow but this time I loaded up and returned my morning stones back to their original place. The joy was in the work!

It must have been a Thursday, Jeannie's half day. I was taking my ease on the toilet just off the kitchen, when Jeannie burst in, whisked me off the seat and with my trousers still round my ankles raced with me out of the house and into the steading yard.

I thought she had taken leave of her senses and howled in protest but my howls were instantly stilled when I looked down the track towards the farmhouse. There against the dike where the hens and the dreaded geese were fed was a roaring inferno.

It was, I later found, an aircraft that had come down on the steep Proncy field and bounced and bounded over the turf until it hit the dike and burst into flames. Mrs Rutherford had just finished feeding the hens and gone back into the house so she at least avoided the fate of the poultry that were incinerated.

Granddad had tried to get to the men but it was beyond any human. He lost his eyebrows and his lovely moustache was ruined and his hands and face peeled and blistered. There was talk of him getting a medal but it never arrived.

On the following Sunday we all walked reverently across the field tracing in the turf the gouges and ruts cut by the doomed plane. We all wept for the two men lost. "Somebody's sons" Jeannie said.

In the late afternoon Jean, Peter and Barbara came home from their day in school in Dornoch and my happy monopoly of my mother was ruined. We were all given our tea and dinner for Jeannie and Granddad was put in the oven. As soon as Granddad came in our mother planted his dinner on the table and headed off to the byre to milk the cow to save Jeanie the job when she got home tired from her long day in the Post Office.

It was one of the perks of the job that Granddad, the grieve, MacAlister, the cattleman and our Uncle Angie (who was married to our mother's sister Maggie) the orra-man, each had the milk from one of the cows.

It was a mighty important perk, for not only did it give us milk but butter and crowdie too.

While Granddad ate his dinner my older siblings shared the table and the lamp to do homework, or to draw or to read, all things I did not know and did not envy. In front of the fire I changed into my nightshirt and waited for Granddad to finish so that I could take my usual place of honour on his lap.

Jeannie arrived in an excitement of iced cakes and while she was retrieving her dinner our mother came back with the shining pail frothing to the top with warm milk. Four mugs were dipped and passed to eager hands and snug in the crook of Granddad's left arm, I sipped the warm thickness, pungent with the tang of clover and the faint whiff of the byre.

Jeannie sometimes brought the mail to save the postie the long hill up to Proncy. Tonight when our mother came back from the scullery Jeannie, with a wide smile, passed her a blue letter. Mother gave a little gasp and all our eyes were on her.

"Is it from Daddy?" Jean squealed.

"Read it to us."

"Give her a minute," Jeannie calmed.

I did not join in all this excitement. A letter from this unknown Daddy excited the other three but I was unmoved.

Finally our Mother gave a little cough to clear her throat and read. It was not the most exciting thing I had ever heard.

"I hope Jim and Al are safe and well". Then a bit about how he could get tobacco but not matches – Granddad tutted at that and sucked more earnestly on his own pipe. His hands and face were better now but his moustache had not recovered.

"And give my regards to your father and to Jeannie," my mother read and Jeannie smiled shyly. "And my love to the bairns."

Her voice stopped but she was still reading and then," They say round here that it is nearly over, that we might soon be heading home."

"Is Daddy coming home?" Could have been Barbara.

"Soon I hope," Mother nodded.

"Are we all going home?" Maybe Jean.

"That soon too, I hope."

"Granddad", I whispered and jiggled myself round so that I could look up into his face, "Granddad, where's home?"

INVERCARRON

My question raised a lot of smiles and I did not know why.

"Invercarron", was the answer.

It could have been Timbuktu or Kuala Lumpur as far as I was concerned. It was a name without a face.

But unlike everyone else in that Proncy room I alone had been born there. That bestows a personal blessing on any place – it lives with us all our lives and comes floating into our minds uninvited and is usually welcome. An accident it is, of course, but it is the first label that life ties to our toe and it is permanent.

The corner of the world, which is Invercarron, is inland West of Proncy, maybe fifteen miles. It lies between the hills, the river Carron and the Kyle. The Oykel, Shin and Cassley feed the Kyle. It is the build up by the millions of years of soft silt dragged down by these rivers, which, when met by the tide driven Kyle, built into a triangle of deep, gluttonous black soil which threw up trees and grass of luxuriant green. The flat triangle was mainly the farm and had also four cottages of which ours was one. On the higher ground, overlooking the Carron, was the Big House with its gardens and a clutch of houses. And between the flat farm and the hill the railway ran alongside the road.

Just beyond our view of railway and road they parted. The railway took a swing left, across the river and straight down to Ardgay. The road got huffy with the rail and carried on with its nose in the air until it met the Strath Carron road and, strengthened by that union, jumped over the river and turned off back down to Ardgay.

It was to save this great loop of road that we used the rail track as our footpath and cycle track.

The railway had come long before my time in the days when the owner of Invercarron House had been a man called Littlejohn. He must have been a strange man if what I was told was true. As a condition of allowing the new rail track to be laid through his land – indeed, quite close to his house, - he had insisted that the station to be built in Ardgay should be called "Bonar Bridge", which named village was more than a mile away and on the other side of the Kyle.

Another of Littlejohn's bright ideas was to insert an "H" into our place name. He was probably upset that one of his letters had found its way to the other Invercarron on the West Coast. So he decreed that henceforth by calling our place "Invercharron" postmen would never again have an excuse for such carelessness. When I was a boy we still had an "H" and Ardgay Station was still called Bonar Bridge.

Some still keep the "H" but I will not trouble with it. In one of the many map redrawing beloved by Councils my birthplace, which like the other Invercarron out West, was in Ross-shire has moved into Sutherland so that should help the posties.

They did not tell me that they had changed the station name. Many years later, at the head of a ticket-buying queue in Euston Station, I caused a major hold-up by insisting that I needed a ticket to Bonar Bridge. It was only when the third or fourth supervisor asked me where this Bonar Bridge place was and I replied "Ardgay" that the problem was solved with much eye rolling and head shaking on the part of staff and queuing public. I slunk off – but happy too that common sense had at long last prevailed and Ardgay Station had come home to Ardgay.

Our house, our particular corner, was tucked away close to the rising ground on which, a little way away and buried in trees, stood the Big House.

There was a gate opposite ours which never closed, which led to the gardens, garage and cottages attached to the Big House. It joined a road, which led from the servant's quarters up to the mansion. There was also a track, which skirted round the bank below the Big House – out of their view – and led to the railway. That was our main road – a quick spin through the woods, a lift of the bike over the railway fence, across the track to the other side (where for no apparent reason there was a cinder track wide enough for cycling). If we were walking we tramped the sleepers. If like me you were small, the sleepers were just too far apart. For grownups they were too close and to step on each second one was just too far to be comfortable. The linesmen who walked these tracks every day were well known for their mincing stride and attracted some unwelcome glances.

There were not a lot of trains. They were steam engined and noisy and if one did come we were warned to lean right into the bank and stay still until the whole train was past. The most feared stretch was the fifty yards or so of the bridge. There the track was too narrow and the walls too close to get out of the way if a train came. We were warned and warned again to listen carefully for a train before we crossed.

One coming north from Ardgay was no danger – we could see away down the straight – but the southbound came through a cutting and burst suddenly from under the bridge which carried the Big House drive. We boys would put our ears to the rail and listen but we were never sure that that was much good. We still had to scamper sometimes.

Just beside that bridge was the best place to watch the trains – the ones heading south. Lie low by the side of the track and the engine hurtled through the bridge arch like a great black dragon in a belch of steam and smoke. And the carriages or trucks clanked and rumbled by and sometimes, if it was a goods train, the guard stood at his van rail and shook his fist.

We put pennies on the line to flatten. But time and again the vibration of the rail would shake the coin off before the first wheel reached it. Or it was clipped on the edge and flew off and we found it on the track with just a nick in the edge.

Then one day the rail was wet and the thunder wheel went right over. We had a penny so flat and thin that it was almost transparent. From then on the Invercarron kids could get as many flat pennies as they wanted – all we had to do was spit.

It was right beside this bridge that we crossed and the warning was repeated and doubly stressed if it was windy and sounds could be mislaid.

If we were heading for school or church we took a path up the embankment and onto the Lower Gledfield Farm road. If Ardgay was the destination the track – a very steep one this time – came out at the fence beside Miss Brown's – almost at the Poplars.

When I first knew these places the Big House had been bought by an Admiral. He was called MacNamara – now in Scottish Gaelic Mac means 'son of' and na means 'of the' and mara means 'the sea'. So he could be very aptly named 'son of the sea'. He looked the part – portly and red faced – he had commanded the base at Scapa Flow in the Orkneys. He had two black labs, one called "Scapa" and the other called "Flow". "Flow" was a treat, maybe a token bark when we met but nothing aggressive. "Scapa" was a terror, she hated bikes, hated people and was generally feared and detested. Father had a tear in his trouser leg to show what "Scapa" could do.

Lady Macnamara was American. She was small and habitually wore Wellington boots, a greasy black beret and a dirty raincoat tied at the waist with string. Our mother was mortified on her behalf –"She even goes to Bonar like that! Just like a tink!" But Lady M seemed unaware that her slovenliness caused concern.

"The main thing is," my father said, "that they allow us to cut through to the railway – so don't go upsetting them."

"But Scapa…." We would chorus.

"Hmmm…" That had him stumped.

"If you see a dog just go like hell," mother suggested.

ROSE COTTAGE

The home, which I could not remember although it was there that I was born, was called Rose Cottage. It was not a very Scottish sort of name and certainly not a Highland one but it was appropriate for the front wall was, in Summer cloaked in rambling roses of red and yellow and the bed beside the front door was a thorny jungle splashed with colour and heady with scent.

The front door led into a glass porch. I can only recall it being used a handful of times, mostly by the minister. The porch was full of geraniums which glowed with pinks and reds but smelled of cats though a cat was never there.

We were joined at the end furthest from the road to our neighbour's house. They were separated from us at front and back by high wooden fences and they proved the exception to the rule that good fences make for good neighbours. War had been declared before I arrived on the scene and there was never an armistice.

No one in Invercarron got on with our neighbours either – they joined in no games and were not included in the free turnip society – though we all suspected they helped themselves anyway. It was a comfort to me that my family was not the only one at war.

There were three bedrooms, the two bigger ones occupied by my parents and sisters and me and Peter shared the smallest at the back. There was a living room that housed a huge metal range that it was the constant duty of all the family to feed. Coal was used sparingly so the regular diet of the range was wood. Winter and summer it was sawed and chopped and carted home from the wood and still its rapacious hunger could not be satisfied.

In the middle of the room was the table. It was my Mother's pride and joy. It was waxed and polished and pampered and rewarded her attention with a golden glow. And it was round. I saw tables in other houses but we alone had a round one. When we ate or threatened to sit round the table it first had to be covered by a blanket and on top of this was laid a wax cloth tablecloth of blue and white squares. When company was expected this double layer was dispensed with and a white tablecloth spread. The edges were embroidered with flowers and the spaces between the leaves and the flowers had been carefully cut out. It was a thing of beauty but such was its dimensions that it did not cover the entire surface of the table - four slim slices of the edge always remained exposed. Mother had it drummed into us that if we should scratch or mark the table retribution would be swift and hard but she could not with manners extend the warning to Aunts and Uncles and cousins so that she was in constant anxiety while we ate until the table was cleared, the guests gone and the blanket and the wax cloth back in place.

All the cooking was done on the range. The oven was remarkable only for its inconsistency. At least that was the standard excuse should something appear from its black maw overdone or sadly sunk. But most of the cooking took place on the top where it was easily watched and constantly monitored.

At the end of the house there was the scullery. Into it led the always used back door and off it was the new bathroom which had followed fast on the installation of running water which came from a tank on the hillside beyond the railway and the road and was always brown with peat but the brown-ness varied with the weather, dark when it had just rained or at the end of a drought when it was nearly empty but usually a tan hue. As well as being brown it was also remarkably soft. Both the scullery and the bathroom were constructed of corrugated iron, which allowed us to monitor the weather without reference to window or door. If it rained we could hear it. Heat and frost we could feel. The only element, which could sneak up on us without warning, was snow.

Extending from the back door as far as the road where it was bounded by a big box hedge was the garden. Flowers beside the path and at the back door - lupins, Sweet William, spirea, peonies, a few more rose bushes and anything else which took my mothers fancy for she was custodian of the flowers and when my father ventured in their midst with Dutch hoe or secetures he was watched and warned.

But the vegetables were his domain. The soil was rich and black, two spade depths he could dig and still it was black and stoneless and gradually as it dried it turned to a deep greyish brown and he defied any thing not to grow there. We had carrots, cabbage, tatties, beetroot, lettuce, leeks, onions and shallots, and cauliflower. Some things he did not bother with. Parsnips, radishes, peas, beans and turnips among them. In the case of the first two none of us would eat them and the second pair were, by our reckoning, just as good out of a can. As for the turnips there was a field of them on the farm and we were allowed to pick one when we needed one.

There were three apple trees. The one nearest the back door was an out and out cooker. It had big, hard fruit that defied even a child to eat it raw. The one in the middle was the "Eater". It bore a multitude of small round red and green apples, which were hard, but they were sweet. Most of them were eaten long before they were fully ripe for to leave them too long was to sacrifice them to birds and wasps. The furthest tree was officially a cooker. It bore grass green fruit shaped like peppers. Though sour they were edible. Those that survived were wrapped in newspaper and stored in the shed and then as if by magic produced on a dark winter night and found to have changed to yellow and to have softened and sweetened. Sometimes they came in from the shed frozen. Then they were sucked rather than chewed but they still bore the scent of summer and tasted of warm sunshine.

Up one side of the garden was a row of black currant bushes and along the top a strip of raspberries. Picking them was a family chore, raspberries were not too bad, and they were satisfyingly large and soon filled a bowl. Black currants, though, were dreadful. You picked and picked and picked and still the bottom of the bowl was barely covered. Whether rasps or currants the picking was hated most for the midges. We ruffled through the bushes and they rose in clouds every one of them angry and very, very hungry.

Rasps were also gathered from the roadside and the railway embankment and then we moved on to the flesh ripping brambles.

But the end result was worth it. Jams and jellies which lasted all through the long winter and promoted earthly bread and scones to food from heaven. Though for sheer scrumptiousness the rasp jam when it was new and not quite set, spread on unbuttered bread or a fresh scone, soaked in and squelched when you sank your teeth into it and we all rolled our eyes in ecstasy and moaned from the sheer beauty of it.

In the winter when a sniff was heard Mother would stick the kettle further onto the range, get a mug and scoop a dollop of black currant jam into it and pour on the boiling water. The steam rose in fragrant clouds and the taste was superb, so without shame we all sniffed and went and got a mug for ourselves.

Behind the house was the Green. It was a big space reaching as it did for the full length of the house and the garden. It contained three sheds all joined. The biggest stored bicycles, ladders and a myriad treasures which my father refused to dump. The next, slightly smaller was where all the tools were kept with cupboards of tobacco and toffee and biscuit tins all loaded with nails and screws and bolts and bits of bikes which might, one day, come in handy. In there too were the boxes of apples and boxes of wax and sections for the bees. The smallest shed had been the lavatory until just before my arrival on the scene and now housed the saws and the axes on which the constant wood production line was based and in there too were piled logs ready for the fire, birch (most highly prized), fir (plentiful but sparky) kindling of used railway sleeper (soaked in tar and desperately keen to burn) and all of them smelt of resin and railways and scoured your lungs and tweaked your nose.

There was a row of Plain trees which separated the green from the field and two pines which were comfortably close to each other and had been joined by a metal bar from which hung the swing, the pit of dust worn below it being evidence of its near constant use.

There was a big bed of rhubarb. The source of even more jam (though some my mother spoiled by adding ginger which only the adults would eat, which might have been their way of ensuring that they did get an occasional taste), of a multitude of puddings and if you avoided the big thick green stalks and went for the slimmer red ones a sharp, tooth numbing snack when eaten raw.

In pride of place were the beehives. Like a row of little cottages they stood facing the road and hummed both day and night like generators and on good days smoked with bees. My father moved amongst them slowly and calmly lifting tops and peering at sections never wearing a veil or gloves. When he finished he would get out his tobacco knife and scrape the stings off his skin - bee stings he assured us would prevent him getting rheumatism when he got old. He did get very, very old but he never had rheumatism whether from bee stings or luck we will never know.

We children, of course, made a bigger fuss when we were stung. Both Mother and Father offered little sympathy, instead accusing us of upsetting the bees and bringing retribution on ourselves. Sometimes that was true but there was the odd occasion when we had suffered an unprovoked attack and not to have that justice acknowledged increased the pain considerably. We were always warned not to pull the bee stings out - to do so simply pressed the little bulb of venom and injected it. So instead we raced for the kitchen got a blunt kitchen knife and scraped the sting off. Then Mother would soften and dip a damp finger in the baking powder and rub it on our wound. The relief was instant and the episode forgotten by the time the baking powder dried and flaked off.

In the early summer the bees ruled a large part of our lives. My father knew when a hive was about to swarm and we were set sentry duties to watch while he was at work.

Thankfully the season of swarms was short. As my father often quoted from a saying even older than he was,

"A swarm in May is worth a load of hay,
A swarm in June is worth a golden spoon,
But a swarm in July is no worth a fly".
The sentry duty was easy enough, one could sit on the swing

and watch, one could kick the ball about and watch and, sadly, one could pick blackcurrants and watch.

It was when the cloud appeared from the hive that action was called for. You howled for help and everyone dropped what they were doing and came running. As the swarm circled and twisted we waited and then, their minds suddenly decided, they would head off and we were in hot pursuit to see where they settled. They as a rule followed a course which entailed any would be follower doing a land bound run through nettles and brambles, under bushes and over fences and dykes. Then to rub salt into the wounds, if their numerous changes of direction had not already shaken us off, they would form their ball in the topmost branches of the tallest tree.

Then it was a case of sentry duty again. It was unusual for them to stay in their first choice roost for long and then when with a hum they were off again it was another cross country run to find their next stopping place.

We were all glad when Father got home on days like that. He would be in no hurry. We would have our dinner first, saving of course the sentry on duty whose dinner was put in the range oven to dry and harden.

Then he would have a rummage in the shed for a sheet and a skip. An empty hive would be slowly inspected and made ready for new tenants and only then, as the gloaming was gathering would he set out to see the swarm. If they were still in the top of a tree they were left there and a quick look in the morning would check on them and if they had not got up early sentries were reset.

If they were in a bush or the lower branches of a tree (sometimes a stroll back to the shed for a ladder was involved) he merely hung his sheet over them, held the skip below them and gave them a good shake. The whole mass would fall into the skip, the sheet laid over the top and a slow calm walk back home.

There the sheet was laid in front of the vacant hive, the skip up turned and given a thump and then the moving mass of bees stirred by his finger until he spotted the queen and she he flicked onto the hive entranced and persuaded to go into her new abode. The rest were left to their own devices and as evening was coming on they crowded in to follow their queen.

All this process was done with no protective nets or gloves and the only tool he used, and then not often, was a smoker. This was a metal topped bellows into which a roll of tightly packed corrugated cardboard was loaded, set to smoulder and the result was a pleasing series of smoke puffs which the bees did not like and could be persuaded to change direction to avoid.

The smoker got him in trouble though. On one occasion after a late evening of herding his bees with the smoker he packed his gear away in the shed and we were all awaked in the night by crackling - the shed was on fire. His roll of cardboard had not been fully dead when he put his stuff away and the smouldering had eventually turned to flame. It was not a big fire. It made a hole in the top of the side of the shed under the corrugated iron, it destroyed his stock of blankets and sheets (essential for any bee keeping operation) and it was put out with a few pails of water from the butt but my Mother reminded Father of it for over many years and he was as a result doubly careful when he put away the smoker.

A WEE BIT OF HISTORY

He must have been planting a bush – something that needed a deeper hole than usual, when in the black, smooth tilth of our garden Father's spade struck metal. He dug it out and threw it towards me.

I picked up a rusty lump of metal and carried it round to the water butt and swilled the soil off. It was undoubtedly the hilt of a sword – barely recognisable but at the same time by size and shape impossible to be anything else.

There can be hardly an acre of Scottish soil which is not steeped with blood. Here in my hands was proof that our wee patch was no exception.

The most difficult problem with history is knowing where to start. The ages of fire and ice and water were memorialised all around us but it just seemed to me to be so very long, long ago.

Then there were marauding Vikings, again so distant from my day that they seemed too far away. But I looked around me and saw the ruined brochs and standing stones by the road, which I was told marked the graves of fallen Viking chiefs - and then it did not seem so far away.

There was a book in the house about the Brahan Seer – if the book was in the house it was there to be read. This Seer was a MacKenzie, Kenneth to be exact, so that brought him closer. He also went by the name of Coinneach Odhar. However many names he had did not help him for, oh!my! – he lived in violent times.

One of his visions was of iron chariots travelling on iron roads. When railways arrived everyone who knew of Kenneth's forecast was mighty impressed. Even more impressive was his forecast that the iron road would span the Kyle between Culrain and Invershin and if that was not spooky enough he saw a line of iron chariots plunge through the broken bridge into the black water of the Kyle. But it got worse – the train in his vision was full of soldiers.

Mother admitted that that bit worried her all through the war but now the war was over there were no troop trains and prospects of one arriving in the near future was nil so she gave the old Brahan Seer zero points. I thought that was unfair, having got railways and trains right and a bridge built I thought he had earned at least nine out of ten.

He saw too the hills strewn with ribbons. Electricity cables one wonders.

The Seer's bosses were Lord and Lady Seaforth, the chiefs of

Clan MacKenzie, and they were not signed up to the health and safety at work legislation. When poor Coinneach Odhar saw problems and scandal ahead for the Seaforth gang they were not best pleased. Not only did they sack him without notice but they popped him into a barrel of tar and set it alight. The poor man hadn't seen that one coming.

These things all came close to us but the Battle of Invercarron was on top of us. The folk from Culrain tried to call it the Battle of Carbisdale but we won't take any notice of that.

I have looked it up and it took place on the 27th of April 1650. Knowing the very day seems to fasten it even more firmly in my mind.

The baddies from the Scottish perspective were the Royalists under the Duke of Montrose who were trying to take over an unwilling Scotland for the usual greedy English king. He had recruited a bunch of Scandinavians and took them over to Orkney and added another gang of Orcadians. They were hoping to pick up support as they travelled victoriously south. But they were not ready to tackle the Sutherlands at Golspie so went off inland to Lairg and then followed the Shin River down to Invershin and across the Kyle there.

But sadly for them the Covenanters had not been idle. Generals Leslie and Strachan were lying in wait at Invercarron but slyly showed only a part of their force. When Montrose saw the weakened enemy he abandoned his high ground advantage and on our flat fields he was surrounded and by the time he realised he had fallen into a trap it was too late for his men to escape.

Montrose himself did escape the consequences of his foolishness but not for long.

He swam the Kyle from Carbisdale Rock and escaped west, disguised as a shepherd, but when he reached Ardvreck Castle he knew he was done and gave himself up to the MacLeods. There is a great story that the MacLeods sold Montrose to his enemies for a few bags of meal. It's a good story but nowadays it is rumoured to be untrue – probably a rumour circulated by the Public Relations Department of the Clan MacLeod.

Poor old Montrose was carted off to Edinburgh. In those days punishments were not done by halves – so having hung him he was quartered and the pieces were sent to Glasgow, Perth, Stirling and Aberdeen. There was no missing the political message!

And then there was a quiet spell in our corner. There was the upheaval of Prince Charlie and Culloden but for the most part that was further south and west. No doubt the people in our corner were affected but it did not write itself large on us.

But excitement came eventually from an unexpected quarter.

A row in the Duke of Sutherland's family up the road at

Dunrobin landed in our laps.

When the old Duke died in 1892 he left a widow and a son and, oh dear! – They did not get on. The widow was the second wife and the heir was her stepson. But she had no intention of being fobbed off with a wee pension.

, Things got dirty. The Dowager Duchess was tried and jailed for six weeks for destroying documents. But she created such a stink that she was eventually handsomely paid off and told she was not welcome on Sutherland land. That took a fair skelp of the country out of her grasp but the Dowager was a tough cookie. She built her castle on the rock of Carbisdale. From her point of view it was the perfect position.

The upstart new Duke and his family could not go in or out of Sutherland by rail or by road without passing her impressive new home.

The castle is not only impressive it is beautiful. It has 365 windows and a great hall lined with white marble statues. On the tower there is a clock with just three faces – the side facing Sutherland is blank, she had no intention of giving them even the time of day.

It was a monument to spite but there was no denying its beauty. We could see it from our door and there were still men around who had had a hand in building it.

Norwegian Theodor Salvensen of the shipping fortune bought the castle and during the war King Olav V found sanctuary there. When the war was done Salvensen gave the castle to the Scottish Youth Hostel Association and it remains the jewel in the crown of that association.

An irony is that when she was banned from Sutherland the Duchess built in Ross-shire. The border scribblers of the latter day council reinstated her to Sutherland by redrawing the border between Sutherland and Ross.

So when we dug up the sword hilt we were not totally surprised. Similar finds had been made in every field all around.

But when I stood there in our evening garden with the rusty hilt in my hands I could not escape a frisson of excitement. Their blood had soaked our soil but they were my people. They were flesh of my flesh and the blood that pumped in my veins was their blood.

RATIONS

"There's a war on", was the excuse for any shortage in any trade even long after the war was over.

Perhaps the city dwellers were aware of shortages of food and maybe children my age suffered for it. But we lived in the country and it was difficult to be short of the essentials there. If beef or pork was in short supply there were plenty of alternatives and there was no compulsion in pulling a hen's neck and the fields were full of tasty rabbits.

On only one occasion do I recall the privations of rationing coming to my attention.

My Mother did a bit of cleaning up in Invercarron House, which by that time had become a private home again owned by Admiral MacNamara.

It was not long after the War and the shop in Ardgay had had a delivery of bananas. These were still on ration and according to the Radio were for families with children though according to Mother at a price, which only an Admiral could afford. The first bunch my Mother saw was in the house of just such.

Whether it was because of the perceived injustice or an uncontrollable desire to give us a treat my mother for the only time in her life to my knowledge became a thief and stole a banana.

It was guiltily taken home and furtively cut into four and we were each given a piece. To her horror none of us liked it.

"It's the last time I go thieving for you lot," she said and she never again did thieve for us. Maybe she thought our ingratitude was a God inspired punishment.

By that time my father was a postie. With a route, which was made up of crofts and farms and gamekeepers, we were never short of food.

Venison, salmon and trout were common gifts from the gamekeepers. The crofters with the odd bag of spuds thrown in bestowed butter, crowdie, eggs and countless hens on him. All were embraced without question except the crowdie.

"Who gave you the crowdie?" was always the suspicious question.

We all knew how crowdie was made, the long kneading by hands which we knew would be clean when the crowdie was made but what worried us was how clean they were when they started the job. We knew some of the women on his round and knew for a fact that hands were not washed; in fact nothing was washed, on a regular basis - if at all.

My father never admitted that he had got the crowdie from Annie Benj or someone of her ilk. It was always Mrs MacLeod or a similar paragon of cleanliness. But we were not always convinced and watched him closely to see that he was partaking of it before we joined in with gusto.

Chunks of venison were pot-roasted – there must have been a million calories in every portion but it was delicious and none of us had ever heard of calories. It might, too, have been sweeter for we knew that most of the time it was clandestinely handed to us by gamekeepers and gillies and the landlords had had no say in the matter.

Salmon came in a similar bracket. Going up the strath on his round my father would be asked by a gamekeeper, "Jackie, would you like a fish?"

Jackie, of course, said 'yes, please'. And on his way back down the strath the keeper would be waiting for him with a fish – a fish so fresh that it was still flapping.

Hens were a regular bonus. Not always as welcome. Those that arrived ready plucked were welcomed with delight – the unplucked ones were not so gladly received. I was useless at plucking and got out of the job. Peter, Jean and Barbara were not so far sighted and took pride in the job, which, of course, resulted in them getting the job to do.

Rabbits always came skin on but Father had been a rabbit trapper so he could skin and clean a rabbit in double quick time. The rabbit pieces were rolled in flour, fried gently and only then added to onions and carrots to make a stew fit to be served in heaven.

Little was risked to the range oven, a few oven scones and the occasional cake. The rest was done where it could be watched. Pancakes and drop scones on the griddle. Salmon and trout in the frying pan along with herring dipped in oatmeal. You may wonder where the herring came from, so do I but they turned up regularly. Salmon was sometimes boiled, with vinegar and salt and left over night in its pan until it could be lifted out cold and succulent and juicy.

Beef, mutton and hens were boiled. They were invariably the centrepiece of the soup, and then became the main course with a load of potatoes.

Soup was made with every available vegetable from the garden with the addition of barley and lentils to give it an extra bit of body. When it was boiled with beef it was beef broth. When mutton was in it was mutton broth. When a hen was the addition it was chicken broth. When there was no meat it was just broth. And they were all superb and eaten with gusto.

The herring were filleted but with skin left on (the skin was good for us, Mother said) were coated it oatmeal and fried. They came out golden brown, crunchy on the outside and white and firm on the inside. We ate every scrap (skin included); it was so good that we forgave the occasional bone.

Salt herring made an appearance too. They were not so good. My Mother loved them and my Father said he did too. The rest of us ate them but slowly, filtering the bones and preparing for a thirsty night and a gallon of water.

There was a group of vans, which did the rounds.

Bowie was the baker. His Scotch pies were to die for but we were never convinced that there was much real meat in them. The same could be said of MacIntosh's sausages and there was a regular speculation as to whether they were as good as Willie Ross's. The result was that we usually had some from each.

Mince raised the same discussions. Mother said that there was more fat than meat in it anyway but none of us had a problem with that. Mince was made with a load of carrots and onions added and then a dollop of that good old filler barley to give it a bit more body and to spread it a bit further.

The really big treat on the gastronomic calendar was the making of a dumpling. It was done for New Year without fail.

Invercarron is low lying. The fields by the Kyle and by the river were regularly flooded in the winter. There had been a lot of rain and the river was in spate and the tide was high. From our window we watched the water advance over the field in front of the house and there was a dumpling boiling on the range.

"What if the water comes and puts the fire out?" I was worried.

"It won't reach here," Mother assured.

But my worry was picked up by the rest of them.

"How long has it got to go?"

"Will it be ruined if it goes off the boil?"

"The water won't reach us," my Mother assured us, though how she could be sure I do not know. But at that time her word was law and the water or we would not disobey. So the water stayed away and the dumpling was raised from its pot, with utmost care the cloth was removed and then it was toasted in front of the fire for a while to let the skin harden.

Slices of hot dumpling, rich with raisins and currants and peel, doused in thick yellow custard. And next day, indeed for several days thereafter, slices of cold dumpling, juicy and judged by some to be even better cold than it was hot – but I did not believe a word of it.

There was no need to go to Ardgay or Bonar to shop, the shops came to us, in addition to the Baker and the Butchers there were at least three grocers. Each household had their favourite grocer's vans. Ours were MacAskill from Ardgay – Mother did not approve of Ferguson's Banana Policy – and MacIntosh the butcher. Bowie was the baker and related to my Mother so he naturally got our trade. Bowie and MacIntosh had small stand at the back door type vans, fine in good weather but not so great when the wind was blowing the sleet and hail round your ankles. MacAskills were the first to get what they rather grandly titles 'A Mobile Shop'. In it you mounted the steps at the back and stood inside the warm, sheltered van.

With what came from the vans, from the postie round and from the garden we hardly knew that there was rationing.

When someone, a visitor from Edinburgh, complained about the scandalous price of eggs my Mother had to plead ignorance – she had never had to buy an egg in her life.

THE BOY WHO WALKED ON WATER

There were two sisters and one brother all older than me. In later life I was to suspect that I was an afterthought. But it did have many advantages. The eldest was my sister Jean, followed by Peter and then Barbara. They were all fairly close in ages but there was a hesitation of about five years before I put in an appearance on the eve of the outbreak of the Second World War.

My brother Peter was about six years older than me and was thus a ready-made protector, advisor and hero.

I was introduced to cycling very early. On the nursery slopes my sisters ran beside me steadying and encouraging. There were no stabilisers and plenty of spills with hurt pride and hurt knees.

Then Peter took over. From the gate opposite ours there was a narrow path, which led steeply up round the top of the disused icehouse and on to the back of the Big House. It was not much used and so narrow that the big beds of nettles on either side threatened to meet. Peter launched me from the top of this hill and all I had to do was steer and balance. The deep beds of nettles concentrated the mind wonderfully. I was a cyclist in double quick time.

He was a scout. They went on camp one summer to far away Culrain (actually it was only just over a mile from Invercarron!). On Sunday afternoon we - Mother, Father, Jean, Barbara and me - set off up the railway line (always the most direct route between A and B) to visit Peter.

We found him shrunken and pale, racked by homesickness. We all pleaded with Father to let him come home but Father would not have it. He was treated to stony silence all the way home and indeed for the rest of Peter's absence.

In retrospect, however, maybe the camp cured Peter's propensity for homesickness for he was later to join the navy and several times circumnavigate the world before settling down to marry and raise a family in Australia.

If I were given any cause for concern at school I reported, with a few additional embellishments, to Peter. He would sort the offender out when next their paths crossed. Andrew Johnson was a bit older than me and for some crime, which I have long since forgotten; he ducked my head under the cold tap in School.

I reported to Peter and was in his company at the Hercher's

sideshows at the Poplars when Peter ran into Andrew. Poor Andrew tried to minimise his crime when faced with a stiff sentence but I was adamant that the attack had been unprovoked and brutal and Peter to my great pleasure agreed with me. Andrew never harassed me again – indeed he remained a good friend for many years but he was always careful to treat me courteously!

There was a group of five or six assorted kids in Invercarron who were sometimes wont to move around together. Like the day we were all going along the shore. Our usual beat was from the river mouth round past the bothy as far as the railway. But it is never easy to abandon a shore – you never know what is just in front and thus it was on a boring Sunday afternoon when we carried on along the shore below the railway embankment towards Culrain. And we were rewarded for there on the gravel was a rowing boat complete with oars.

It was clear that it had come adrift from its moorings and come ashore on our shore. It had probably come from the Balblair side but we were not in the business of finding out who it belonged to, we were in the business of clambering aboard and getting it afloat.

Peter and Harry were the biggest, oldest boys so they took the oars and made a fair shape at it. Enough to take us down the Kyle to nearly as far a Bonar before turning and heading back.

We made a big effort at dragging the boat up into the line of trees and camouflaging it with branches and bracken.

The next evening we were back and the boat was relaunched. Down the Kyle to nearly Bonar and then turn to head back but this time the tide was in full ebb and progress was slow. And then disaster struck – we became firmly stuck aground on a sand bank.

We were well aware that the middle of the Kyle was full of shifting sandbanks. They were filled by birds and seals every time the tide went out. But such had been the excitement we had a communal rush of forgetfulness.

It was a decision for the leaders and we followers cowered in the bottom of the boat while Peter and Harry, with advice from Barbara and Marion, came to the conclusion that one of our number had to get out, thus lightening the boat enough hopefully for it to float free and then the plan was that with that accomplished we should approach with caution and pick up the volunteer and retrace our path back to shore with all possible haste. Our situation was open to inspection by any one travelling out the Lairg end of Bonar.

Peter stepped from the boat and pushed us off the sand. He may have been a wee bit over strength with the push for we shot out into deep water and he was left standing on the submerged sandbank in the middle of the Kyle. A car stopped on the Lairg road and a couple got out to stare at the boy who appeared to be standing on the water.

A second car stopped and a man got out. We were galvanised into action. The oars were manned and the boat skimmed back towards Peter. A leap added to a large dollop of luck brought Peter off the bank and into the boat and with renewed energy and urgency we headed back towards our secret harbour.

For days we lived in fear of discovery. It hardly seemed possible that our escapade had been witnessed without someone telling one of our parents. Maybe the prospect of explaining that they had seen a boy walking on the water was a discouragement.

But our arrival back in our harbour had been spotted by Hughie Matheson and he must have got word to Balblair that their boat was on his side of the water for the next time we screwed up courage to set off for another cruise we got to our harbour but the boat was gone. We all tutted and swore and cursed Hughie for an interfering old bastard but I know that I was rather relieved that we would be spared any further groundings or worse. I suspect that I was not the only one.

Our parents never heard that story until we were all grown up and even then my Mother nearly had vapours just thinking of it.

Before the electricity came the lamp was king. The usual favourite (my Granny had one in Bogan and so did my Granddad and Jeanie in Proncy) was a Tilly. They were tall and rather elegant. The fuel tank formed a solid brass base – always polished – and a long thin column rose to carry the mantle within a globular shade.

We were not a Tilly family – we were for an Alladin. A much more lamp like lamp and I liked to think a much more pleasing name. The base was a fluted tracery of metal that led up to the fuel tank on top of which stood the wick and the mantle with a tall, clear funnel of glass.

The mantles were of such fragility that the lamp, when it had to be moved, was carried as one saw them carry glycerine in films. It came, covered with a film of wax, in a wee cardboard box. And when fitted had to be set alight to burn off the wax and then it stood there white and delicate, made of ash it seemed.

For the most part the lamps behaved themselves but they were capable of moods. For no apparent reason they would start to pop, or flare or fizz or decide to smoke. My Mother was a match to all those whims.

We could have been to Granny's or maybe to Proncy but where ever we had been it was dark when we got home. Peter had not been with us (school maybe) and was not in when we got home – nothing unusual in that, as soon as he was home he was off down to the steading. But he had made an effort to welcome us home – he had lit the lamp.

We came into the living room and my mother gasped and we all groaned. The lamp was a feeble, silver patch and all else was thick, thick black. A blackness you could feel, a blackness that hung in dripping streamers from the ceiling, a blackness that caked the walls and every other surface with a glistening layer of oily soot.

The lamp had smoked. Whether it had done it from the moment Peter had lit it – hurrying to get down to the horses and cattle – or if it had cunningly waited until he had turned his back, we will never know.

I trembled to think what Peter's reception would be when he did get home. There was a selfish frisson – we all have them – of being fireproof while our hero walked unknowingly into a blistering firing range.

But I was wrong. His mortified return was greeted by a conciliatory hug from our tar-streaked mother and tears were wiped into streaks of black.

By the time Father got home the clean up was already underway. Moving the tar took weeks, months even, and gallons of soapy water and even, eventually, paint and still Mother would pause in her work, lift her head and sniff and sigh. "I can still smell that bloody soot!"

USDEAN

Usdean and Marie came with their three children to rent a farm cottage. They had come from Skye and spoke with the soft accent of the Islanders who spoke Gaelic as their first language and soft pure English as their second.

Usdean was not a farm worker. He drove a lorry for Tawse at the quarry at Ardchronie and Invercarron was to be a temporary stop for them but however temporary it was it turned out to be a boon for the Invercarron children.

Marie was a gentle woman who missed her Skye. She would smile shyly and say "When I hear that song," she was referring to the Skye Boat song, " When I hear that I have to cry."

Like Marie Usdean was soft spoken and gentle but he was a big, muscular man and he worshipped children. He drove his lorry, laden with stone, all over the north and usually he had a child passenger. When his own children were in school he would beg a neighbour for one of their younger ones and I was lucky to be his most available passenger before I went to school. He had cushions on the passenger seat so that his young companions could see out of the high cab.

He treated his young passenger with respect, as if we were people his own age. It was a meeting of equals. We talked about things we saw in the fields and what people were doing and why. If we had a question he would listen carefully and give it some thought before giving a careful reply. It was not unknown for him to say that he did not know. "Too deep for me, Uilleam."

We went over the Struie one day and coming down the other side above Alness and Invergordon the Beauly Firth opened out before us and it was full of ships.

"The Home Fleet," Usdean said and stopped the wagon.

I was speechless – I had seen pictures in the papers of these great, grey floating castles but here they were lying before me in ranks, in numbers.

"They're the aircraft carriers, the big ones." Usdean was pointing. "And that and that, they're destroyers and that beauty there is a cruiser. I spent my time on a cruiser."

"You were in the Navy?"

"Aye," Usdean grinned. "Able Seaman MacKinnon."

"Did you go places?"

"Aye, I went places," he seemed sad as he spoke. "America and Russia mostly – a different life it was."

"Different life?" I didn't understand.

"Ach, it's ancient history." He was happy Usdean again. "Is that not a sight to stir your heart?"

"Aye," I said for that was exactly what it was and I was never to see such a sight again for the Navy deserted Invergordon and the firth became a place of memories.

We went into the Railway Station in Dingwall one time – that was a trip to foreign lands for me – and he supplied pennies for a crane machine until I had captured two bars of chocolate. We ate them with relish on the way home.

When I accompanied him in his lorry we sang a lot. He taught me, parrot fashion, Gaelic songs – usually soft, sad airs.

"Grand, just grand!" he would chortle when I got a verse right. "Let's have it again Uilleam."

I would pipe the song and he would nod and smile.

"When we get home you come over and sing that to Marie."

And after tea I would go over the field and Usdean would call me in.

"You listen to this now," he would say and stand me beside the fire facing Marie.

Proud of myself and desperate to do my teacher justice I would sing.

"Beautiful just!" Marie would cry and wipe tears from her eyes. "Sing it again, Moi Gloule."

And I did.

One evening he made a couple of runs in his lorry, the cab stuffed with every child in Invercarron, to his work place at the quarry. There in one of the Nissen hut sheds we all sat on the floor, the lights were turned off and in a flashing, whirring fantasy we saw our first films.

They were jerky, they were black and white but they were magic. All were cartoons and we shrieked in awe and screamed with laughter. There was a break and we were given lemonade and cakes and then the lights went off, this time we knew what to expect so we cheered, and away we went to heaven yet again.

Usdean had in his younger days been a heavy competitor in Highland Games. Word got around and some of the young hopefuls from round about persuaded him to coach them.

This offered us evenings of excellent entertainment. The group gathered in the wee park beside our green and we ignored the midges to sit out along the fence to watch. The events were hammer throwing and caber tossing. For the latter my father had found a nice straight trunk,

"Not too heavy," he said.

Sometimes Usdean would demonstrate a point and whirl the hammer and send it flying.

"You should be going to the games yourself, Usdean," my father said to him when he wandered into hearing distance.

Shyly, as if caught being a show-off, he came over. "No, no, Jackie," he smiled, "I have the knack but the speed is gone."

"I haven't seen any of the lads throwing that far," Father said it quietly, their secret.

"They will though. If I can get them right with their feet and their hands they'll knock spots off me."

"Are any of them any good?" My father asked doubtfully.

"Bobby and Alistair have a lot of promise," Usdean said. " They are trying too hard just now – if I can get them just to get the movement right they could be very good. Now all they want to use is brute force and that's just grand once it is in the groove but it's getting it in the groove that's the problem."

To our sorrow the MacKinnons did not stay long in Invercarron. They got a house in Bonar.

The last time I saw them was early on a New Year's day morning – probably about two or three o'clock. I was home on leave and Peter was on leave from the Navy so a boisterous New Year was in prospect. We would have brought the New Year in at Jessie's and then wended our way to Usdean's.

Marie opened the door nervously but laughed with delight when she saw us two peering at her.

"Come in. come in," she cried. "Look, Usdean, it's the boys."

Usdean stood up as we went in. He seemed smaller but his smile had not diminished. He wrung our hands and Marie got the glasses.

Drams were drunk and wishes made and Usdean said,

"Give us a song, Uilleum."

Peter bridled. "Don't try Gaelic, " he hissed. He thought it an insult for me, a non-Gaelic speaker, to try to sing to Usdean and Marie in their mother tongue.

"Away with you!" Usdean laughed at his objection. "Are you thinking I did not teach him the words properly?"

Peter knew when he was beaten and shrugged and I had the confidence of a dozen drams so launched in,

"Cailin mo ruin-sa is leannan mo ghraidh,
Ainnir mo chridh-sa 's I cuspair mo dhain,
Tha m'inntinn lan solais bhi tilleadh gun dail,
Gu cailin mo ruin-sa is leannan mo graidh.

"B'og chuir mi ealas air leannan mo ghraidh,
'S a rinn mise suas ri'sa ghleannan gu h-ard,
A gnuis tha cho aoidheil, lan gean agus baigh,
Is mise bhios cianail, mur faigh mi a lamh."

"Gur tric sinn le cheile gabhail cuairt feadh an ait,
'S a falbh troimh na cluaintean gach bruachag is magh,
Na h-eoin bheag le smudan a' seinn dhuinn an dan,
'S toirt failte do'n mhaighdinn d'an d'thug mi mo ghradh.

"Bha mise lan aoibhneis nuair fhuair mi cheud phog,
Bho'n chaileig ghrinn uasail tha aighearach og,
'S e mo mhiann is mo dhurachd, cho fad 's bhios mi beo
A bhi posd' ris a' ghruagaich tha suairc agus coir."

"Was that right?" Peter asked dubiously when I was done.
"Word perfect," Usdean glowed.
"Beautiful just!" Marie was weeping. "Sing it again, Ma ghoul."

And I did.

GLEDFIELD SCHOOL

I was the baby of the family. Far enough behind my close grouped siblings to be almost certainly an afterthought, if not an outright mistake.

It ensured a cosy childhood for me – I had two sisters to coddle me and a brother to look up to and to fight my fights when the enemy was too big or scary for me.

I was late going to school. I suppose that the end of the war and our move back home and the return of our father all happened when I should have been sent off for my first day. Perhaps they just forgot and I was not so keen as to push my case. Whatever the reason I did not enter the world of academia until I was six.

Jean and Peter had moved on from infants and Barbara started in the big room as I entered the small one.

Our Gledfield School was a two room, two teacher place. The infants were put into the care of Flora, a wispy woman who cycled every day, rain, snow or shine from Culrain to give us the groundings. The Big Room was the realm of the head master, who, when I first darkened their door was Mister Smith, a grey faced disciplinarian. By the time I left to go to the big school in Tain, Mister Smith had gone and my namesake Mister MacKenzie came and he had the same grey, grim look as Mister Smith and we knew at once that he was not a man to be treated lightly.

But it was Miss Flora MacKay who took us new arrivals into her care. She had a range of ages but it was in total not a huge gathering though it was at times confusing.

There were two other new arrivals on the day I started, Betty from Invercarron, who I knew like a sister, and Fergus from Ardgay. We were issued with our wooden framed slates and slate pencils and set to copy the shapes of letters and numbers and no matter how well we drew them they were instantly wiped clean and the whole thing had to be repeated.

For recreation from engraving into the slates we were given Plasticine and made lots and lots of snakes and worms. Occasionally we were given a piece of new brightly coloured Plasticine to add to our stock and then for a little while we turned out pretty marbled snakes and worms but it did not take long for it all to change back to brown.

Around us the older children chanted the times tables and we absorbed them through our skin – an osmosis of learning – and as our elders chanted we mouthed the chorus too. When the older ones got spelling we picked up the basics too. It was not long before I knew that "I" was always before "e" except after "c". We got wise too that there were trick words, which Flora slipped in to liven proceedings – they usually had a 'ph' or started with cunning 'w'.

Every week we had a visit from the minister – one week it would be the Church of Scotland man and the next it would be the Free Church fellow. They both failed to make great impressions for we were mostly already well steeped in religion and they did not have a lot new to tell us. Never a day passed without a prayer and a hymn or a psalm and come Sunday most of us were trooped to the service in the morning and then sent back in the afternoon to Sunday school. Catechism was learned and repeated and the Bible was fed to us in regular helpings.

Not as bad as Achnahannet though. That was a single teacher school and the incumbent was a religious zealot called Miss Brice. She had a handful of pupils whose days were dominated by Bible reading and study with a liberal sauce of prayer. The most prolific contributors of children to Miss Brice's classes were the Wilsons, who managed a steady annual succession of sons. All the boys developed in later life into hard, drinking, fighting men who could clear a bar single-handed and often did. Quite what that has to do with Miss Brice I do not know – but it struck me as interesting.

We had another weekly visitor, Mister Little, a small, plump elderly man who came to teach us music. Music began at singing and ended at singing, which was fortunate for me, for in those years of unbroken voice I was good. I could sing like an angel and adults were as putty when I hit a rich seam like the time at a prize giving when, buoyed by the prospect of the long summer holiday, I had given a real belting to "Linden Lea".

Mister Little may have had many talents but the ones, which impressed us most, were his ability to play the piano with two hands and, if the occasion merited it still keep the tune going with one. The one handed operation came into play when he had one of us boys stand by his stool and try to render a solo. While he accompanied us one handed the other strayed round behind us to urge us ever closer and to gently stroke our buttocks. It did us no damage and we suffered no lasting harm and, perhaps, we made old, lonely Mister Little happy.

Some of the songs we sang, mainly in a disjointed choir, confused me mightily. There was one which had the most mysterious and boring chorus ever heard.

"Oh, gin I were where Gaddy rins,
Where Gaddy rins, where Gaddy rins.
Oh, gin I were where Gaddy rins

At the back o' Ben Achie."

At the time we were given no explanation of why this chap Gaddy was so persistently chasing Ben. And if we used that spelling or pronunciation in Flora's tests she would have had an apoplexy.

At Christmas we got a new selection of songs but they were no less confusing. One got off to a bad start in the very first verse.

Apparently the singers lover had sent him a Partri Juniper tree. Why one would give someone a Juniper tree for a Christmas present puzzled me mightily for years.

Then, being Scottish, we had a few warlike chants- again full of spelling mistakes. "Scot's wha Hae" and similar recycling of battles long ago. And there were nonsensical jaunty things like "The wee cooper wha lived in Fife". The only Cooper we knew was Willie and he lived in Mid Fearn.

There were a couple of boat songs too. There was the Mingulay one, which was the rowing song as dead Kings of old were rowed across to their graves on the Island. That one gave us the beat of the oars and hence our first lesson in rhythm.

And there was the Skye Boat song. We all approved of the bravery of Charlie and Flora as they ventured across the stormy ocean while their enemies quailed on the shore, "follow they would not dare".

I was less impressed and rather disappointed to find, much later, that you could stand on that shore and almost spit over the sea to Skye.

Another of my blossoming skills, which Flora spotted, was drawing – particularly drawing daffodils. I was given a big sheet of drawing paper and drew hundreds and hundreds of daffodils. They were easy. A downward pointing arrow in green represented the stalk and the leaves. A side on capital "T" in yellow created the flower. Individually they might not impress but repeated en-masse they were spectacular. I even took the thing home and spent my evenings creating daffodils. When the foreground was massed with flowers I made big green clouds for trees and big white trees for clouds. The finished work went on the classroom wall – a worthy reward I modestly thought.

At some stage on my journey through Gledfield the milk and the dinners arrived.

The milk came daily in little bottles with an inset cardboard top in the middle of which there was a wee perforated flap. Press it down and insert a straw and hey presto!

We had our milk at eleven and most days that was easy. But some days – the hot still days when the windows were wide in a vain attempt at catching a breeze – then the milk was drunk as soon as it was delivered and even then it was not soon enough to prevent it being on the turn. But we were none of us prima donnas – many a time we had sour milk and thought little of it. There were no refrigerators and even if you put the bottle in the sink the water from the tap was never much below the ambient temperature.

In the winter, the stove in the middle of the room glowed and crackled as if it was about to take off, but its heat did not reach our desks. When icicles hung down the windows and our breath was a mist, then the crate of little bottles looked like a case of candles. The milk stood tall above the top of the bottles and the wee cardboard cap was a toorie in an icicle.

Then the crate was parked within reach of the stove and twirled with her foot by Flora every time she passed it. We only got to drink it when it was time to go home and it was still even then too thick to come through the straw so we just swigged it off and crunched the crystals and enjoyed it fine.

At the back of the main building they built a canteen. I cannot remember it being build so I would guess it was either beamed down from space complete or built fast in the summer holidays.

Isobel appeared like the building – she was suddenly there – a cooking goddess. At home there was a diet of broth, main course was the bit of beef or mutton, which had been boiled in the broth. Potatoes were always boiled as was the accompanying turnip or cabbage or whatever was in season in the garden.

And puddings were always milky – tapioca, rice, sago and so on – sometimes with boiled rhubarb, which curdled the milk, or stewed apples and failing that a spoonful of jam.

At school we were introduced to roast meat and roast potatoes. Peas were a daily menace as they skidded off the fork, and we had stews with pastry on top, which they called pies but we were a bit puzzled by that – all Bowie's pies were round.

School puddings were the big treat. Sponges with dollops of custard, tarts and pies. We were all entranced and each of us had a favourite – mine was a sort of king size bakewell. It had a layer of pastry with a thick spreading of jam and on top a deep, deep yellow sponge. It sets the taste buds drooling after sixty years.

It was during the tenure of Mister Smith that the boys were led out into his big over-grown garden and paired off and given a plot to dig. It was to be our introduction to gardening – and as Mother said when she heard, "Got rid of some of Smith's weeds".

I shared with Hamish and neither of us was impressed by Mister Smith's demonstration of digging. Our respective fathers thought nothing of double digging our black Invercarron tilth. Mister Smith was demonstrating a shallow turning of the soil which buried the weeds but little more. We did not question the method – one questioned Mister Smith at one's peril.

So we all planted a little row of potatoes, a row of peas, lettuce and carrots and then went off home on our summer holiday and came back to a crop of weeds and half a dozen tatties when we did finally dig them up.

It was on that day of tattie lifting that Mister Smith went off on one of his many daily visits to the house leaving us in the garden. Hamish and I helped ourselves to an apple each from his tree. True to his form he returned just as we took the first bite from the forbidden fruit. The apples were so sour that they were uneatable. Mister Smith's view of justice was to make me and Hamish throw away the apples – which we were about to do anyway – while he reached up and gave an apple to each of the other boys and insisted that they eat and enjoy.

The lesson, which we actually carried away, was that both guilt and innocence could leave a sour taste in the mouth.

THE SQUARE

The greatest boon of living in Invercarron was that the farmer was Duncan Munro and he allowed – nay, encouraged – the boys to help around the place.

Peter spent practically all his waking, non-school hours down at the Square as we called the steading and I was soon tagging along, getting in the way but learning.

The unlikely centre of the Square was the turnip shed. Slap in the middle it spent most of the year empty and was the natural meeting place. It was where jobs were handed out – and pay packets. It was big enough for furious football kicking and even when all the turnips were brought in and piled against the back wall there was still room for a kick about.

The turnips were of two kinds. Yellows were piled against one wall and Swedes – pronounced to rhyme with Teds – on the other. There was a mingling in the middle where the two piles met.

It was understood that the turnips were available to all. Our Mother would shout after us to bring home a good swed.

I took home a Yellow one time – I was still untrained – and for the next year the request to bring home a swed was always tailed by " and see that it's not a damn yellow."

In the Summer the turnip shed was empty. The floor was compacted soil and dusty but ideal for no holds barred football with a big leather ball which could had the consistency of a cannon ball – no side lines, belt it against the side wall and the ball was still in play. The demarcation of the goal at one end was easy – it was the big, in summer open, sliding door. At the other end the goal was a notional space on the wall equivalent to the size of the door – it made for some heated disputes and exchanges, which sometimes came close to blows.

There was in the turnip shed a demonic machine. It was the turnip cutter – bung a turnip in the trough, pull down the weighted handle and the turnip slices shop out the bottom into the waiting basket. Boys were warned off – but, of course, we used it. Then in one of the great leaps that the arrival of electricity brought, an even bigger more deadly machine was installed. Turnips were thrown up into the big hopper at the top and below there was a vicious rotating drum of razor sharp blades that shredded the poor neep into strips in double quick time. We boys were double warned and this time we steered clear – the top was too high and more importantly it made a hell of a din so that the whole square knew when it was on.

"An accident waiting to happen," old Duncan said sadly as he watched Jim pushing down on the turnips which had got jammed in the hopper.

Sure enough Jim later lost a slice of finger and spent near an hour going through the shredded turnip before he found the missing piece of digit and went off over to the house to call the doctor to make an appointment.

There was, also in the winter turnip shed, a big drum perched on concrete blocks with a tap at the end. It was full of treacle. It was for the pampered stots feed – the ones destined for the fat stock show in Dingwall. The treacle made their coats shine. Of course, we boys took out the top bung and dipped sticks into the black, black interior and drew out pungent sweetness, which we dribbled into our mouths.

"You boys will have a right shine on you," Duncan would chuckle, "and a right dose of the shites to go with it."

On either side of the turnip shed there was a byre with stalls, which were dusty and empty all summer and rich with cows and calves in the winter. Bedded in deep straw, each bovine body radiated heat and the byres were the warmest place on a cold day.

Beyond the byres there were big folds for wintering stots. They started in the back end on bare ground and could hardly reach the feed troughs but by their own efforts and piles of straw come spring they had to kneel to reach the troughs.

Then the steading paused and allowed an alleyway before the last building at the side. One was probably a byre at some time but now it was sectioned into small loose boxes where the pampered beasts were coddled and at the far end a couple of pens for pigs.

At the other side of the square there was what had been the stable but only stalls remained and for most of the time there was only one horse. That left room for yet more stots and at the far end, in solitary splendour, there was the bull.

Above it was the hayloft. Packed full up to the rafters in winter. It was dark, narrow and prickly with scents of summer when I crawled along the little triangular space between the high rafters and the roof. Scary, too, when perhaps, I thought, there was no room to turn, no way back. Who would ever look for me up there? I would be found at last when the hay store dwindled but that would be too late for me.

The thought was enough to supply the sweaty energy to work back the way I had come and peer out the end door, high up, and rejoice in the prospect – death defied again!

All these sheds were end on to the big yard between the

steading and the farmhouse. And all these sheds, except the turnip one, led into the long barn which stretched from end to end – maybe sixty, seventy yards – and which held great banks of straw. Great for hiding in and just digging in like a mole.

Above the barn and stretching the whole distance was the granary. The number one place for rat hunting – stealthy up the stairs and throw open the door and watch the exodus and let Scotty scoot between our legs with a howl of delight. He would get a couple every time and sometimes, armed with a fork, I would manage to corner one but most times when it turned and showed its teeth I carefully left a wide enough space to allow an escape route.

Across the floor of the granary after harvest there were huge beds of oats or barley. Not quite reaching the sidewalls these beds of grain was perhaps a couple of feet deep and maybe thirty yards long. These banks of grain had to be checked regularly for heating and every few days two men undertook one of the heaviest jobs on the farm. All those tons of grain had to be shovelled a few feet to turn it over. They started at the end, transferred each shovelful behind them and worked all the way down the granary. It was a nightmare job and none of us boys were daft enough to try that one.

Behind the high stone building of barn and granary there was one more two-floored addition. It housed the threshing machine and the bruiser. The stack yard was just yards away at the rear of the steading so it was not a long trip to bring the sheaves from the stacks and fork them through the big door at the top of the threshing shed. Inside, level with the floor, was the feed slot where the sheaves were sliced open and fed, grain first, into the twirling threshers. The man who fed the thresher stood in a wooden pit so that the floor was at chest height. It was another place of threat to hands and fingers but happily no one succumbed.

The thresher and the bruiser had been driven by a pulley to a tractor outside but with the arrival of the electric they both changed to that source of power.

Old Duncan was never wholly happy with the electric. "It's sitting there fizzing away all the time – it's too damn closely related to fire for my liking."

There was a grey fenced transformer in front of the steading and he would stand, with head cocked, listening to it hum. Later, he did not pause to listed but as he walked past he would crack his stick against the fence and snarl, "Shut up, ye bugger!"

As the thresher spewed grain out of the wooden slots at the side into hession bags, the straw was tossed by big wooden fingers into the barn and with forks and grapes dragged along so it filled the whole back of the barn and was handy for the byres and the folds. The chaff shook down in a great drift under the thresher – that was a weekend job for me. Fill the barrow with the dusty chaff and wheel it into the fold and dump it. The stots sniffed and sneezed and galloped around like daft bairns. It was a dusty job but not heavy – the barrow weighed far more than the chaff – and there was no time limit.

I could do it as fast or as slowly as I liked and if Duncan should come out to the square he would watch me for a wee while and say "Well done. Lad." And then go off back into the house.

The bruiser was a more responsible job. There was a chute from the loft down into the bruiser hopper. It was my job to feed the whole grain down the six-inch square hole in the floor. Too much and it would overflow the hopper down below – too little and the rollers on the bruiser would start grinding metal on metal and there would be a shout from below and maybe angry footsteps on the stair.

Running along the back of the barn building there was the cart shed. Well-spaced pillars of stone held up a sloping roof. In the horse and cart times this was where the carts and horse implements were lined up. Now there was only one horse cart. The rest was taken over by tractors and their accoutrements.

There was a 'Case'. Squat with great wide mudguards on the rear wheels where we juniors were able to balance and cling on. The other tractor was a 'Farmall'.

Great, big skinny thing with hardly a mudguard to speak of. The seat was away up in the air and the steering wheel shaft sloped down for miles and entered the long bonnet half way along.

The 'Case' was easy to drive – I had to sit right at the front of the seat to reach the pedals and maybe have to slip right off sometimes. The 'Farmall' called for contortions. I sat behind the gear lever and reached up above my head to get a hold of the wheel. But it was the bigger machine so it was worth all the bother.

The tool shed was at the back too. A crashing corrugated iron place piled with metal bits and pieces most of which were forgotten and probably not recognised but Duncan kept then in case…

There were drums of oil and fuel and grease in there too, giving it a stink of factory.

Hamish and I took a tin of grease through to the turnip shed. Donald, who worked on the farm at that time, was not our favourite and at that moment must have offended us even more than usual. His bike was leaning on the wall and we carefully greased the handle grips and the seat.

I am sure we did not expect to escape some retribution and we did not need a second warning when Donald saw and pursued us the next day.

We split and my luck was out. Donald followed and collared me. He dragged me – protesting, of course, my innocence – into the tool shed and liberally clarted me with grease.

When I limped home my mother screamed when she saw me and set about scrubbing me with, I thought, more than necessary vigour.

There was, needless to say, a trial. I did what any sensible criminal would do – I pled not guilty.

"But why would Donald do such a thing?"

"Someone greased his bike."

"Oh, ho!" Mother was seeing the light.

"Not me", I cried. "Not me. It must have been Hamish."

"And was Hamish greased?"

"Donald caught me. Hamish got away."

My Mother was procurator Fiscal. If she saw that there was a case worthy of a higher court the evidence was passed to Father. And we all knew that he judged that if Mother saw the case as strong enough to reach him it was just a case of passing sentence.

I got away with the greasing. Maybe the red eyes and splotchy skin were judged sufficient.

There was an unexpected bonus in having got my punishment over quickly. Hamish was still skittish and watchful, knowing full well that he was still on Donald's wanted list. And naturally he was ambushed and greased and I told my Mother and she said, "So the real culprit has had his comeuppance! Just you see and steer clear of that rascal Hamish – he only gets you in trouble."

To tell me to cut off Hamish was like telling me to cut off my arm, I knew that and I am sure Mother did too.

"Yes, Mum," I said.

THE TURNIP

"Boring. Boring, boring! The bloody turnip must be the most boring plant on God's earth." It was Watt having a say while the hoeing team edged its way across one of Invercarron's big fields.

"Yes, and more bloody work than anything else," Geordie agreed.

Eric stopped and looked up at the sky. Behind him Watt, Geordie and me also had to pause.

"What y' looking for?"

Geordie had vainly scanned the empty blue sky.

"Flying pigs!" said Eric. "You agreeing with Watt."

Everyone except Watt and Geordie laughed.

It was true that Watt and Geordie did not see eye to eye on many things. They were not often in the squad together for neither enjoyed the hoeing. But Geordie was employed by Invercarron and had to come up with a good sheep related excuse to be absent. Watt, like some of the other neighbours, needed the services of the Invercarron bull.

To me it seemed strange that this feud should exist between two men who looked so alike.

Both were in their sixties and of portly figure, with round faces and big moustaches. Both were similarly clad, even when hoeing – the uniform was hairy tweed plus-four suit complete with waistcoat, long knitted hose and heavy, tackety shoes with upturned toes. Their mutual nod to more casual attire for hoeing was that the shirts were collar-less, although ready with the studs in place, and there was no tie.

Their uniformity collapsed when it came to headgear. Watt wore the gamekeeper's compulsory fore and aft, and Geordie sported the wide flat cap of the shepherd.

Both hats were, of course, of tweed!

Watt had served in the first war and Geordie, I was later to learn, had not. This may well have been one of the causes of friction.

Watt had a habit of regaling us with stories of foreign lands. These did not go down well with Geordie.

"What were you in the army, Watt?" someone asked.

"I didn't make it past Corporal," Watt would admit sadly. "I wasn't officer material."

"No. I mean what job did you do?"

45

"In the cookhouse likely," Geordie said softly but loud enough for all to hear.

"Keepers were in demand," Watt ignored the comment. "A man who could shoot was treated with respect."

"Were you a sniper?"

"I did a spell at that, a bad business," Watt said sadly.

"He wouldn't like shooting at something that could shoot back," said Geordie and spat.

"Did you kill anyone?" I asked.

"Some bloody sniper if he didn't," someone said.

"Losh, no, boy," Watt laughed. "We were just firing blanks, - it wasn't for real."

They all laughed and I was disappointed.

"Did you kill anyone, Geordie?" I tried again.

"Geordie kill someone!" Watt laughed. "With his flat feet!"

And they all laughed except Geordie and me.

But both Watt and Geordie were not wrong this time. Turnips were lots and lots of work. From the usual ground preparation they needed drills and then the wickedly round seeds were sown a few a few drills at a time. They were wanted in succession for the hoeing. Then when the seedlings were through the round-shouldered drills were scaraferred to slim them down to hoeing dimensions.

Then I came into my own. It was one of the few jobs at which a competent boy could do a man's work.

Maybe that is why I remember the hoeing as fun, as opposed to Watt and Geordie's opinions. And maybe, too, that is why I see us hoeing always in the sunshine.

There must have been days when it rained and was drab and muddy and, perhaps, boring. But the passage of years has washed those days from memory and in recall all those days were sunny.

I do remember one year that I was sent forth by a thoughtless mother in my usual short trousers and by the end of the day the backs of my legs were so sunburned that I could scarcely bend my knees. So there! It is not just a trick of old age memory - the sun really did shine in those days.

The end rigs were the training grounds for us novices. Holding the hoe more than halfway down the handle we would laboriously spend an hour after school doing a few yards.

Old Duncan would look at our work when he was passing and - is it that sunshine thing again? - I can recall no criticism but only praise. I had a good teacher. Peter was a master with the hoe and won prizes. Long after when Peter was home from leave from the Navy Old Duncan would greet him with a shout "Give that man a how!"

And having mastered the rudiments we sharpened our hoes and entered the Hoeing Match.

They were held annually, alternating each year between the Poplars and Invercarron.

We kids had three sections of drill each - no more than thirty yards long. We painstakingly smoothed the soil and laid each turnip smartly at right angles to the razor sharp drill.

Occasionally, of course, the plant, which should have stayed, decided to follow its siblings and throw itself to its death, which left us artists with a space where no space should be. With a swift twitch of the hoe the corpse would be retrieved and pushed back into its allotted spot. If the day was damp and the judge came early the subterfuge would be un-noticed but if the day was hot and the judge tardy then the wilting dead plant betrayed us. We kids were judged first - which seemed only proper then - but now I realise that it was a cursory look before he went on to the serious business of judging the adults.

Old Duncan always accompanied the judge - who was always one of his many cronies - even at the Poplars where he did not have the same proprietorial rights as he did at Invercarron. In latter days I suspected that accompaniment of the judge might have something to do with us Invercarron kids winning so regularly. But that might be a wicked slur on the integrity of Old Duncan and on the judge. We Invercarron kids probably really were the best.

There was an endless prize list at those matches. As well as the usual first, second and third in every age and sex section there were prizes for the first finished; the last finished; the youngest; the oldest; the most recently married; the most recent father (or mother); the furthest travelled; the best local; the best from Caithness; the best from Sutherland; the best from Ross-shire; the best from Kincardine; the best from Criech. And I have probably forgotten a few. One had to be very unremarkable and very unlucky to escape winning a prize for something or other.

Finally I was promoted from doing end rigs to be tagged onto the end of the regular squad.

The squad varied from day to day. Permanently in number one position was Duncan's son. The full-time farm workers, including the shepherd if he couldn't find a good enough excuse to be elsewhere, followed him. Then there came the crofters, mostly old men who came for a couple of days hoeing or harvesting in return for favours - one of which was sexual, for their cow would be brought annually to the Invercarron bull. And last in the line came me.

At the end of each long drill there was a pause while pipes were filled and fags rolled and while they waited for me to finish. As soon as I arrived they were ready to start again and the injustice of that, which meant that I got no break between drills, has stayed with me to this day. But there was a couple of longer breaks - the half yoking which no longer depended on the horse it was named after - when flasks were produced. Being the junior I was usually sent along the end rig to fetch the piece bags from the last stopping place. On a few days of exceptional heat or just because he felt like a blether Duncan would arrive with bottles of beer. I was allowed one - warm and frothy like used bath water - but I drank it with pride.

And there was always the talk. Some of the older men had been in the first World War and we got yarns about foreign places and foreign people. Local scandal was inspected and dissected. National politics was discussed and dismissed. Occasionally they would forget that a kid with big, flappy ears was tailing them and discuss more risqué subjects and tell tasty tales. Old Watt was good for the more exotic tales of far-flung women. "Lord, boys, you should have seen the ones without teeth".

"That's gross," someone up front muttered.

And another time he was on about a blonde he had met.

"Very amorous, blondes."

"What about redheads?" Some one up the front asked.

"They say redheads take awful easy," Watt said.

"I heard that too," Eric joined in. He was one of the younger crofters and he had a reputation as a ladies man.

"You would know."

"I had a red headed lassie in Oban a few years back," Eric said and added wistfully, "I often wonder...."

If Hughie was with us these sorts of subjects were soon quashed. Hughie was a Wee Free and didn't like that sort of talk and would snort and spit and eventually raise my presence as an excuse for censorship. (I used to try to be present when he brought his cow down to the bull, you could tell he didn't like me being there. He didn't like being there himself.) I didn't like it when Hughie was on the squad but he was only a couple of days man so he didn't often cramp my colleagues.

Hoeing was not the end of the turnip saga. Come the back-end there was the backbreaking job of clipping them. This employed a blade about a foot long with a wooden handle at one end and a hook at the other. Between these extremes there was a slightly curved blade. The idea was that the hook pulled the turnip from the ground but in fact I never saw it used. The men would grab the turnip by the shaw, pull it up, and slice the clipper through the base to take the root end off and then another slice to remove the shaw. Bearing in mind that one hand was holding the shaw and the clipper blade was invariably razor sharp, this was a perilous exercise. Consider, too, that much of the time this weary occupation was carried out in cold and rain.

Happily this job did not coincide with any school holidays and the daylight was short so boys did not do the clipping – it was doubtful that we would have been allowed to wield such a dangerous weapon.

I did manage sometimes to get on the tractor and pull the trailer down the field while the full-time farm hand threw the turnips into it. If it was a single-handed job there was a lot of energy and time wasted jumping on and off the tractor, moving a few yards, throw and then move again.

The turnips gathered were destined for the turnip shed.

A lot of yellows – maybe more than half the field – were left in situ. They provided winter food for the sheep. A net fence ensured they ate one section at a time and only when they had cleared that section was the fence moved to let them onto a fresh plot. With the addition of oats the sheep did very well though when there was little left but the very bottom bit of the turnip I often pitied them. In the mud they looked dirty and desperate and in the frost, when their hooves tapped on the solid ground and the turnips were like ice-lollies, they looked no happier. It is not in a sheep's capabilities to look happy – I think it is their devil's eyes

PAT

During the war there had been a large number of Canadians billeted around Ardgay. Their main purpose was to fell trees. They also took away, when they went home, some of our womenfolk – two of my aunties among them. They also bequeathed a smattering of bairns who joined the local schools shortly after me.

They had cut a great swathe of trees off Invercarron Hill but a lot still remained. It was when they were being felled that Pat arrived.

Pat was a small man – invariable attired in navy blue overalls, a tweed jacket and cap, crunchingly heavy boots and khaki puttees.

The most remarkable thing about his ensemble was, however, not his attire but his two companions. He brought to be stabled at Invercarron two huge Clydesdales – not old beasts but grey and white so that they looked venerable in both size and colour.

It was Pat's job to get the felled, trimmed tree trunks down the hill to the roadside. It was cruelly hard work for man and beasts.

My father and I were passing one day and watched him and his team come down the hill. The horses strained with arched necks and Pat danced behind with long reins, singing out instructions and encouragement and all the time dodging the swinging, crushing tree with alarming agility.

"Hard work!" my father shouted to Pat when he got close enough to hear.

"It is so!" agreed Pat with a laugh.

The horses were stabled in Invercarron steading but Pat had got himself lodgings in Ardgay. Each morning and evening the two great horses thumped past our garden gate on the way to and from work.

When we were in the garden (usually picking accursed black currents) Pat would give us a regal salute from his perch sideways on one of his horses.

"His legs are too short to reach over a back that size," my Mother said. "Indeed, no one has legs long enough to straddle on of them giants."

Later Pat would cycle past on his way home. Again he would salute but the gesture lacked the regality of his former greeting. His bike squeaked frantically – "Has he never heard of oil," my mother would sigh - and he pedalled laboriously with his boot heels on the pedals.

We were astounded when in one of our concerts in the Ardgay

Hall the predictable local, loved turns was interrupted by the announcement of "Patrick O'Kelly". No one knew whom to expect and there was a ripple of laughter and a sharp intake of breathe when, dressed in his usual working togs, onto the stage walked Pat.

He took position in the centre of the stage and stood rigidly to attention. His eyes were fixed on a spot well above our heads on the back wall of the hall.

Suddenly a fiddle began to play off stage and Pat began to dance. It was such a dance as we had never seen before. His hands were tight by his side and his head and his eyes never moved but his legs and his heavy booted feet moved like lightening. The beat of his boots was fast and furious.

Most of the male audience was made up of tackety boot wearers –crofters, farm hands, shepherds, keepers and boys like myself – and we gazed open mouthed as this tiny man translated our humble footwear into a musical instrument – thing of beauty, a work of art!

Pat and the music stopped suddenly and the silence was utter and deep for a few seconds and then was broken by a roar of approval and shouts of "More!"

Pat allowed himself a shy glance at the audience, the merest suggestion of a smile and a stiff little bow and turned and walked off.

We cheered and whistled but Pat was a subscriber to the 'leave them wanting more' school.

For weeks, for months, we boys, if we came across a likely board or an echoing floor, would freeze our bodies and try to 'do a Pat'. But, though we made a noise and we sometimes suggested a beat, there was none of us who could successfully imitate Pat.

"It's bloody hard," we would say in disgust as we stumbled, "You must need to be Irish."

Pat went away – "Someone died in Ireland", my father said – and his horses were loosed out in the wee field beside our green. They stood together down at the water trough, still and shy. "They're missing Pat," my mother said. It was a grey day of smoor, which could not make up its mind whether to be rain or mist.

The next day was a day of sun and heat. I was lolling on the swing when the earth shook from the beat of thunderous hooves.

The horses were prancing round the park, tossing their heads and kicking their dinner plate hooves into the air. I ran across to the fence to watch. They charged round a few times, snorting and whinnying and then, as if on a signal, they threw themselves down and rolled around kicking their heels in the air.

When they rose they shook themselves and looked around shyly as if making sure that their madness had not been witnessed. Then it was that they saw me, open mouthed and bewildered. Almost apologetically they came slowly over and towered over me and dropped their heads over the boundary and I stroked them and they riffled their lips and I felt the soft velvet of their noses.

Then I was off, running like a mad thing past the back door and into the garden. I grabbed two apples off the first tree I reached – big green cookers that smelled of Autumn.

One of the Clydesdales still stood with his head on our side of the fence. The other was yards away, sniffing a thistle disapprovingly.

"Here!" I held forward one of the apples. The nose twitched and the lips gently opened to reveal teeth like a set of dominoes. With slow care he bit, avoiding my nervous fingers and with a crunch and a splash of juice half the apple was gone, being crunched.

The remaining piece of apple was lifted from my palm by tactile lips.

The crunching chewing had brought the other beast to me and he leaned against his brother and his soft lips explored me until I took the other apple from behind my back and it was gone, picked from my hand and crunched whole.

I was off again like a whirlwind, past the back door with two more apples.

My mother had seen my swift passage and when she saw the horses she came over. She watched as I fed each. "That's enough", she said when I threatened to head off for more supplies. "They're hard, sour things – we don't want to give these boys belly ache."

And she began to pet the huge heads. Smiling into the soft brown eyes and saying things like "Aren't you just lovely," "oh, so handsome!" and "My beautiful," and they nuzzled their noses into her.

Pat was only gone for a few days and he and the horses went back to their hard graft and Autumn changed to Winter and still they pulled frozen logs down the hill.

On Saturdays the team did not work. I heard that Pat liked a few drinks in Fergie's on a Friday night so he was not up early but hangover or not he still faithfully pedaled up and spent most of the day combing and brushing his charges.

"What's their names?" I asked.

"They don't need names," Pat replied from under the belly of one of the horses. "I know who they are and they know who I am."

"Can I brush?"

"Help yourself."

"I start where?" I looked at the mountain of horse before me.

"Brush out the long hair round the hooves, you'll reach that!"

"Will he kick?"

52

"Don't worry, he likes to be brushed so the last thing on his mind will be to kick you."

Gingerly at first I brushed the long, white tresses and then, ever so gently, the hoof was raised an inch or two out of the straw.

"There I told you he would like it, " said Pat.

I was enormously flattered that such a regal beast should find my trifling attention to his liking.

I was, like Pat, there most Saturdays at that time and I liked to think that the horses knew me.

Then one day they did not pass up the road to work. When I got home from school my mother told me that one of the horses was sick. Of course I wanted to go down to the square but it was already dark and Mother said, "If Pat's still there he won't want you hanging about."

When my Father came home and was told about the horse he said, "I wondered why there was a light on in the steading".

"Poor Pat must still be there," Mother sighed.

When my father had finished his meal Mother handed him a bag. "There's a flask of tea and something to eat. Take it down to Pat. I don't think he has been out of that stable all day."

Father went and was gone a long time.

When at last he came home I was in my pyjamas but I had managed to put off going to bed until he came back.

"What's happening?"

Mother was asking as the door opened.

"The horse is in a bad way," Father hung his bonnet on the back of the door. "I doubt it will make it through the night."

"And is Pat staying there?"

"He won't move. He's sitting in the stall with the horses head in his lap, soothing and stroking the poor beast."

"Did he eat?'

"He was very grateful for the tea but said he couldn't eat. That's why I've been so long. He finally agreed to eat a little bit to please me and then he finished the lot."

"Thank God, " Mother said, "Now off to bed you."

The horse did die in the night and I and Mother cried over it in the morning.

Then suddenly Pat and the other horse were gone. I never heard where they went. They went as quietly as they had come. But still, if I wake in the darkness of the night and listen hard, I can hear the thud of hooves and the rhythm of dancing boots.

HAY

Haymaking is the most nerve-wracking time of the year. No other operation is so dependent on the weather. It is a huge gamble. Once the decision to cut the hay is made and carried out there is no going back. The cut grass lies in the fields and dries – weather permitting.

An odd wee shower is not the end of the world but a summer deluge can be the end.

There are machines designed specifically to whiffle the damp hay and let the sun and the breeze do their job. Before these machines made their appearance the turning was done by a row of men and boys equipped with forks.

The timing of the hay cutting was pivotal to many ground nesting birds. The main dweller and nester in the hay fields was the corncrake. Thankfully then the haymaking was late enough in the year to allow the young corncrakes to fledge and flee before the vicious blade of the mower arrived. When farming fashion changed from hay to silage the entry of the mower into the fields moved forward and that was fatal for the corncrakes. Then, however, that tragedy was still in the future.

When the hay, lying in strips as left by the mower and the whiffler, was considered dry enough the rake was brought in and the hay gathered into more concentrated strips. The first rake I remember was a horse drawn one.

Hay, I always thought, was the most difficult harvest to handle. It had a mind of its own. The tools did not seem to help the situation. The two-pronged fork was useless – it was like handling peas with chopsticks.

Once the hay was in coils - small stacks dotted across the field – the worst of the danger was past. A downpour could do damage but not to the previous extent. Some crofters put little caps on their coils – a square of canvas or a flat cut plastic bag – but in the bigger fields like Invercarron it was just a question of getting it into the stack yard as fast as possible.

We boys really wanted to be on the tractor but some old guy like Watt got that job and we were called to higher things – building the load.

It was actually quite a tricky job. The same disorganised nature of the hay which made the building of coils difficult was multiplied ten fold when transferred to building the hay load to survive the journey across the field and into the stack yard.

The trickiest part of the journey, the test of our trailer loading skills, was the gateway out of the field. The gateway was rutted and as the load went through it swayed and we the builders were still on top so we had a double interest in it getting to the stack yard in one piece.

The building of a haystack was an even more challenging job – especially with Old Duncan snooping around making sure the stack was straight and true – a credit to his stack yard.

The loft in the square above the stable was packed too. That was a hot, dusty job and the height of the rafters made tramping it in a job designed for small boys rather than men. We sneezed and itched and sweated and packed and gradually worked our way to the fresh air of the doorway.

But the vast majority went into the stacks. Enough to keep sheep and cattle going all through the winter – a sweet smelling store of clover and grass bursting the winter chill with summer sunshine.

And because the hay was so wayward to load and collect there was always a spread of bits and pieces still lying in the field and that grieved Old Duncan.

As long as the weather stayed dry he wanted all the hay in. And that was a job for the horse, the rake and a boy. I was cock-a-hoop when he asked me. The men harnessed the horse for me, I couldn't lift the collar never mind get it over the tossing head, and hitched her up to the rake and off I went.

We crossed and recrossed the field gathering the scattered leftovers. I sat on the iron seat high above the rake and twice on each crossing I leaned precariously out to pull the handle to lift the tines. The result when the job was done was to be two neat rows of hay, which could be easily collected and gathered in.

The horse needed little direction. She plodded from one side of the field to the other without much reference to the proud pip-squeak on the iron seat. Had she objected there was little I could do. She was a big beast, with powerful feathered legs and feet the size of dinner plates.

But in every Eden there is a serpent. In my and the mare's little bit of heaven there were the clegs. They swarmed round the horse and boy. Boy could bash them when they bit but horse could not. So at every end rig we paused and I clambered down from my perch and went round her squishing them. Her skin trembled where the clegs sucked. She was a greyish red colour which made her look old but she was young enough to have a spark of the devil in her and she was not above having a little tap-dance and that was when I had to look lively too to avoid the dinner plates.

To add to her tendency towards skittishness the mare had one blind eye which resulted in a lot of head tossing - and her head was as hard as her hooves and was best avoided. She was perpetually anxious about what was happening on her blind side so as I squished the clegs on that side I had to keep up a monologue of assurance.

Between us we had the clegs mastered but we came close to disaster when a hornet came to look us over. When the mare heard the staccato buzz she pranced and danced and stood up on her hind legs. As a result there was no dignified climb down for the boy - I jumped.

There were no onlookers but if there had been they would have been entertained by a dancing horse and a boy running round her, flapping his arms and panicking.

The episode was brought to a conclusion, not by any action of horse or boy but simply because the hornet buzzed off. It took us both a long time to settle our nerves and assure each other that all was well.

The job got done and Old Duncan was pleased and gave me, I think, a fiver. Big money but I would have done it for nothing.

AUNTIES GREAT & SMALL

If ones wealth were to be measured in aunties I would be up there with the Multi Nationals.

I can reckon on fourteen – four each on my mother and father's sides and then another half dozen by marriage.

There were an equal number of great aunts but I was too late for most of them and only a few floated into my ken, beings from another age, another planet.

Annie was the best known to me of these great aunts.. She was tall and frail with her thin grey hair safely secured by a net. She wore useless rimless glasses for with glasses or not she could not see. The blindness today would have been a matter of a quick hospital visit but Annie cruised her gentle way around the furniture in Proncy and then sat by the fire looking with her white eyes at the ceiling, lips sometimes moving, as her fingers traced her novel across a mighty book. This was not brail, this was moon print and the books were huge, like books of embossed wallpaper samples.

She could determine between light and shade. I, to my shame, crept back into the living room where she was sitting alone reading and sat silently watching her. I cannot imagine what I expected to see her do, it was the sort of thing that wee boys do. I sat still as a statue for an interminable time and then, as she turned a page, she said, "Are you not away with the rest of them?"

"Peter went off without me" I lied and skulked off out to sit on the horsie.

Annie's surviving sister Kate could not have been more unlike her. Where Annie's face was small and neat with perhaps the merest shortage of chin, Kate had a square bold face, with a hawk nose and a big wide chin. Not only in appearance were they at variance. Annie was the gentlest quiet woman you were ever likely to meet whereas Kate would pick a fight in an empty room – and win.

When she retired from her housekeepers job in Edinburgh she returned to live in Dornoch.

She had a succession of large floppy Labradors. When they were black she called them - in those days of non-politically correct speak – "Nigger". When golden they were named "Goldie". She did not have an original thought in her head when it came to christenings. I can remember two "Niggers" but only one "Goldie" and it was "Goldie" which still breaks me out in a cold sweat.

Auntie Kate had come to visit. We children were warned and double warned to be on our best behaviour. We could tell that even our mother was nervous. When Kate looked at you through her thick lenses even the bravest flinched. She was so short sighted that she leaned right up to your face and her eyes were huge and relentless.

Peter and I were nominated to get out of harms way by taking "Goldie" for a walk. "Goldie" was nice enough in a roly-poly way. She was amiable and probably quite stupid.

We went down to the river and waded across to the Gledfield side. Near the mouth of the river there was a deep dark pool referred to as the Boat Pool. The Gledfield side of the pool was, for a distance of maybe fifty yards, edged by a steep concrete wall. I did not know it then but know it now that this was part of the great Telford strategy when, in the early 1800s he built the first Bonar Bridge. To replace the ferry with one bridge instead of two necessitated the rerouting of the Carron so it entered the Kyle further west than previously. Hence the big, concrete bank across the Gledfield side of the Boat Pool. In what turned out to be one of Peter's not so bright moments it was decided that we would persuade "Goldie" into the water at the lower end of the pool and let her swim to the top where there were steps up which she could land. "Goldie" was daft enough to go along with this and started swimming up stream. But some way short of the steps she began to slow and we urged her on. Our urgings took a frantic turn when her head bobbed under and she came up snorting water.

She made it, of course, or I would not be here today to tell the tale. We grabbed her collar and yanked her out. She lay gasping on the steps and it was a little time before she could be persuaded to walk and then the recrossing the river at the shallows made her nervous.

To our shame it was not the welfare of the poor dog that worried us it was the prospect of going home and breaking the news of her demise to Auntie Kate. If Kate didn't kill us our mother would.

Kate and her dogs were well known in Dornoch. She habitually walked them on the golf course, and they were all keen collectors of balls. When they pinched one off the green, the players got very angry.

Auntie Kate was serene, "Such language" she would snort, when she reported the incidents "They certainly were not gentlemen".

To her credit Auntie Kate, when she retired, went off by sea to visit her brother Donald in Australia. Donald had served in the first world war and when he was given the choice of a demob suit or a plot of land in Australia he plumped for the latter. He married there and had a family so there was another great aunt who I never knew.

Many, many years later when Peter was in the Navy the submarine on which he was serving surfaced for a few days in Melbourne. Peter got leave to go to Mildura to see this long lost great uncle. By photographs he found a man very like his brother our granddad, large boned, tall and thin. His face, though was deeply tanned. On his head he wore a tartan cap. When he and Peter sat below a big gum tree in his yard Donald whistled the first few notes of "Scotland the Brave" and the birds in the tree mimicked his whistle and gave a ragged rendering of the song. He had, he said, spent many months teaching the birds the song, maybe even now there are birds in Victoria which give occasional renderings of "Scotland the Brave".

Peter asked him if he missed Scotland. Donald smiled and looked around his rolling acres of vineyards, "Are you kidding, boy?"

There was another Great Aunt much closer to home. She was the wife of my Granddad's brother Duncan. Mary was another maker of scones and jam and to visit them required a day of fasting before we went. The great attraction at Uncle Duncan's was that right beside the house there was a burn. It was made for damming and diverting. "Don't get in the burn," Auntie Mary would warn and we made straight for it.

When Uncle Duncan was sent out to fetch us for our tea he always knew where to find us.

They even called their house "Burnside".

My mother's Auntie Meg lived in Edinburgh. I can picture a small, stout woman but then I think that I never actually saw her. Though there must have been a photograph glimpsed somewhere. I did, however, know her husband and their two children. Their home in Edinburgh was a useful halfway house and, over the years, they got used to putting up a MacKay or a MacKenzie for the night.

George was the surviving head of the house. He was a huge man with massive hands and a big, square head. He worked for Alexander's buses, and often made the journey to Leyland to bring back to Edinburgh the bare chassis of a bus. He perched high above the engine, open to all the elements.

When he got it back to base Alexander's would build the coach body, and the new bus would appear in blue with a big blue swallow and the slogan 'Take the Bluebird".

George would be called upon to travel in these exposed conditions all year around and wrapped up with goggles and a pilots helmet he must have resembled a giant yeti. He told us all tales of blizzards round the Devil's Beeftub but he had to tell us each story an average of three times – it took us that many tries to understand his thick Edinburgh accent.

Annie and Kate, Meg and company   were sisters of my

maternal grandfather. On her paternal side only one great Aunt survived, she was known as Nana. Goodness knows what her correct name was. If I was ever told I have forgotten.

Auntie Nana lived up behind Bonar in a long, low croft house, which looked out over Loch Migdale. Nowadays English buyers would be queuing up for it and crying "Look, dahling, just look at that heavenly view".

To me the main attraction was that in the right season sea gulls nested on the hill behind and I could go up and collect a hankie of eggs. Auntie Nana did not wholly approve of my harvest. She felt a duty of care to the gulls that made their homes so close to her own. So when next Spring came I was warned before hand by my mother that if I should find any eggs they be left at the bottom of the garden and be collected on the way home. As Nana stood waving at the doorway there can be no doubt that she saw me collect my white bundle. When I said so to Mother she said, "It's not the same – you're not rubbing her nose in it."

Of my ungreat aunties, Jeannie stood out. She was the anchor of the Mackay side. She had not married and she looked after my grandfather until he died and Annie in her last years. Brothers and sisters from all over the world came home to visit and they always stayed with Jeannie.

She worked for years in the Post Office in Dornoch. There must be something in the air in Post Offices because so many of their minions can be sharp. There was no question that Jeannie was sharp. She did not suffer fools gladly. She gave Kenneth pure hell, but if anyone dared say a bad word about her little brother she would make them regret opening their mouths. She inherited the MacKay eyes and wore glasses of boggling thickness. Her hair was always in a bun and we young ones never questioned that Jeannie would be there for us. Romance, we would have laughed at. But long after she died I found out there was a love. She would wander softly away on a Proncy summer evening and it was assumed she was taking the air after a stressful day in the Post Office. But there was a beau in a nearby farm. They even went away on a holiday together. When I heard it, I was stupidly pleased.

The eldest of the Mackay sisters went away in the wartime to Canada. Another lived closer but might have been in Canada for all we seen of her. The youngest married an asthmatic crofter and worked the barren land of Rogart doing her work and often his and they fitted in enough time to have three children. In between was my mother. She was a little nervous of Jeannie and courted her good opinion. We were warned to be good when Jeannie was about but, in fact, Jeannie was blind to our faults and we all remember her as our greatest childhood friend.

Occasionally Father hired a car from Davy MacKay in Ardgay and we all headed off to visit Babs and John in East Langwell. John owned a very smart Hillman with a wooden steering wheel and leather seats. He showed it to Dad with pride. "What's the Ford like?" he nodded at our hired car.

"I find the steering awful heavy," Father said.

"You're used to the wee Morris van," John laughed.

And we all acknowledged with canny smiles that Dad could twirl his wee Post van on a sixpence.

Electricity and mains water had not reached East Langwell. The toilet was among the trees at the front of the house. We all tried not to go but were fed with so much tea that we had to give in. Mother was practically cross-legged before she gave in.

"It's a few eggs," Babs would say as she passed my mother a shoebox of eggs wrapped in pages from the Farmer's Weekly.

"Oh! You shouldn't," Mother would say and accept the box.

"And here's a few lamb chops and a bit of mutton leg," Another heavier package was slid across the table, "We killed a beast last week so there is plenty."

"Lovely," said my Mother.

"That's a nice car Johns got," Father offered as we left and he gave a wide berth to the parked Hillman.

"If it came to a choice between a nice car and a stinky toilet I know which I would close," Mother said and we all wrinkled our noses and agreed.

Our way home would lead past Proncy and we could not pass there without calling in. Letter of our arrival would have warned Jeannie but we were always later than we had intended.

"My word what time do you call this?" Jeannie threw the door wide and we all trouped in.

Granddad was sitting by the fire. He was even thinner now. His face a skull with a stretch of pale parchment drawn across the bones. Even his moustache seemed to droop. But shyly we climbed up on his knee, Barbara, and me with the precedence of being the youngest. Jean and Peter smiled and envied us.

Our Mother leaned over us to kiss her father. She meant to say "Oh, my love how ill you look," but instead she said," Are they feeding you?"

Granddad laughed her concern off and we snuggled into him and felt the sharpness of his bones and wondered at the size of the skeletal hands, which circled us.

"Auntie Annie gave up on you," Jeannie said. "She's up to bed."

"Oh shame, " Mother cried.

"Go on up she'll be that glad to see you."

Mother led the way upstairs. Jean and Peter were following so we youngest ones wriggled down off Granddad and followed.

Auntie Annie was sitting up in bed. Her glasses were gone. Her hair stuck out from her head in little grey pigtails, like a modest Medusa. Her hands were busy, feeling faces, "How big" "My word what a big boy" and we wriggled under her tactile scrutiny.

"I left a penny for each of you downstairs," she said. "Ask Jeannie."

"Say thank you," we were unnecessarily prompted before we could say a word.

Jeannie gave us each two half crowns.

"One is from Auntie Annie and the other is from me. And Granddad," she added like an afterthought.

Five shillings! I had no notion of how to spend such wealth and no shops to offer suggestions so I took it to school on the following Wednesday and gave it to Miss Heap for my savings stamps. They nearly filled a whole page.

It was late when we left Proncy.

There was tea and scones and pancakes and sponge cake of deep yellow stuck together with an ooze of homemade rasp jam. "Have another slice."

"No, no I'm full."

"Granddad'll have it," I said. Granddad was still by the fire and I think he only had a wee bit scone.

"Are you hearing that?" Jeannie loudly.

"Yes, I'll have a bit if it's going spare, bring it over boy and help me see it off."

I took the plate over and shared it bit by bit. Mother and Jeannie exchanged smiles and I did not know why.

It was time for off. Jeannie planted two parcels on the table, "Its just a bit of butter and crowdie. The hens are off the lay so I haven't an egg."

"Oh, Babs gave us eggs. Have some, they're in the car."

"No, no our ones will be back laying any day now. I am surprised the Rogart ones are doing so well."

"They'll be getting corn and they have the steading to shelter in." said Granddad.

"That'll be it, " said Mother and Jeannie together.

Then we were back on the dark road, piled in the back of the car fighting off sleep.

On Reevag Brae the car slowed and Father pointed up the hill to our right,

"See, she's still up," he said.

"It's awful late," Mother said.

"We canna pass her road," my father said and at Whiteface we turned up the hill to Bogan and Grannies.

The curtains were not drawn – she had no need of curtains, no neighbour lived within a mile, so she saw the lights coming and was at the door when we stopped and sleepily tumbled out.

"What a time to come," Mother shouted.

"Ach, come away in, it's not late," Granny ushered us in. "What a mess, you've caught me doing a bit of painting."

She had several tins of different coloured varnish, a bunch of brushes and a sponge. The walls were wood interlocking boards and they had been green –"I'm just fed up o' green", and she was working the colours into wood pattern, the veins with knots and all.

"What work," Mother cried.

"You'll have a cup of tea, just in your hand."

Protests were ignored and we were given a cup of tea in our hand and after a deal of rummaging Granny found a tin with biscuits. They were concrete hard and we bit and wondered which would give way first, biscuit or teeth. Happily the teeth won and we knew then why they were called snaps.

The framed photographs, all of kilted soldiers, had been taken off the wall while the decoration work was in progress and were lined along the mantle piece. Father, Davy, Donald, and Peter.

Granny did not sit. Father her eldest son was guided into her chair and she wandered round beaming on us all and casting admiring glances at Father, hanging on his every word and nodding so vehemently that all of her little black wrapped body joined in.

"I'll just see to the dishes."

"That you will not. I'll get them done in the morning."

"I'll put them through though," and we all trooped into the scullery and put our cups in the sink and looked at the shining pails of well water with their thick wooden lids.

We were off again , this time really the last leg. As we turned off the track down the hill we slowed. Granny had gone back in and we could see her clearly in the lamplight as she remounted her stepladder to get on with her interrupted work.

"It's after midnight," Mother said.

"Aye, she's hardy," Father said proudly.

On my father's side there were three proper blood related aunts. One of them, shown in a photograph as a small sharp woman with tight angles and wild hair, went off to Canada and sent mother, and the other relations, literature from the Jehovah's Witnesses. "Bloody check!" my Mother said.. Another went to the Black Isle and she too was beyond the pale. That left just Cathy and Janet. A living reproduction of her mother Cathy was warm and hospitable be you adult or child. It was unthinkable to run a message to Cathy and expect to get out with out tea and a scone or maybe a pancake.

Janet was the widow of the Sergeant Jack MacDonald who died on the same day as my uncle Donald at El Alemain. She soldered on and raised her son and her daughter and was true to his memory and trust.

On her wall was a huge framed photograph of Jack – "Shona got it done in Dingwall" – showing the tall, maybe a wee bit arrogant, Kilted Sergeant at ease with his rifle sloped and his head turned to the camera with a faint smile.

When we left Mother paused and wiped a tear away. I looked at her wondering why she should suddenly weep as we went to get the bus.

"He was from Kirtomy, you know. Up by Bettyhill," she said and I did not know if she was really speaking to me. "Soft spoken, and oh! So handsome"

And from that day on I had my standard of 'handsome' imprinted with a picture of Jack MacDonald.

Of the aunts who gained their dubious place by marrying my uncles there were some I did not know. There was one in Canada, one divorced and disappeared, one off to Australia and one in Raasay who I never met.

On my father's side though, there was one star. Jessie had married my Uncle Donald – he who was drowned in a loch in Glen Affric when the bank below his lorry fell away – and had two star sons who were to become my greatest friends.

Jessie could play the piano and, poor soul, was press ganged into accompanying the various efforts at local concerts. She played the organ in the church too and for a time played in a dance band.

She thrived on music but her most superb instrument was seldom aired - it was her contralto singing voice. It was sometimes heard when the church singing faltered but it was later, much later, when New Year was very new and drams were flowing with Rossie, Peter, Spirrak, me and Jessie that she would give her rendering of the "MacDonalds of Glencoe". She was a MacDonald and gave the song her all, tears flowed and not just hers.

"Daft," she would say after. "Nowadays they have massacres of thousands but we peasants still shed a tear over a dozen. But it was not what was done – it was how it was done."

The other star auntie married my mother's youngest surviving brother Alick. He was the wartime Commando. It was while training in the mountains of Snowdonia that he found, in Criccieth, a golden treasure.

Mattie was reddish haired, freckled and beautiful. When excited she would plunge off into Welsh and everyone loved her. When Hamish brought her home all his sisters fell for her at once, all the children followed her about and got under her feet and howled with laughter when she chided us in Welsh. Auntie Annie hooted with shrill laughter at the things she said. "I love making crowdie," she said one day as she came in from the kitchen wringing her hands, "It makes your hands so clean." Poor Auntie Annie howled with mixed horror and laughter.

I first met her when I was five and she was a rock for me for more than sixty-five years. She died on New Years Day 2010. She was buried on a Welsh hillside beside her Al.

What joy would have been in heaven that New Year. The saints would be smiling and even God himself would be grinning – at least he had got his works right this time!

BIRDS

In the springtime Hamish and I spent every spare moment bird nesting. We tramped and climbed and peered and tallied.

There were strict rules. To count we had to be able to see or feel that there were eggs or young in a nest.

The likes of seagulls' nests were not counted – they were too easy and much too numerous. The see and feel rule also denied us rooks nests in the treetops, or herons or woodpigeons. Similarly swallows, swifts and house martins were disallowed. And though we could see sand martins sweeping in and out of their holes in the riverbank we could not see or feel so could not count.

And there were things like tits that nested in ridiculous places. In the fence along the railway there were cast iron strainers with holes for wire to go through and they had hollow interiors. Blue tits went in through the wire holes and nested at the bottom of the dark interior. We could hear the chicks chirping but we could not see or feel, likewise the sparrows that found their way under slates on roofs and made plenty of noise but did not up our tally. And trotty wagtails, who strutted all over the place, avoided our census by building in the dykes – the only way to get to them would be to demolish the dyke and Duncan would have had something to say about that.

Bearing all these self inflicted strictures it seems a wonder that we had a tally at all. But not only did we have tallies but they were big ones – we each reached over two hundred and in one year Hamish broke the three hundred mark. Of course we were not both allowed to count the same nest – which led to occasional questions of the reliability of one or other of our memories.

Some of the Ardgay boys were bird nesters too. The first time we heard them bragging about their score they were talking about forty or fifty. We soon put them right and thenceforth their numbers when we were in hearing distance were measured in the hundreds. Hamish said "They're lying bastards."

I agreed, "Lying Bastards!"

There was a long drive to the Big House and it was bordered all the way by huge rhododendron bushes. These were choc-a-bloc with nests. Mostly it was blackbirds. Neat and well made with splotchy eggs but they were no match for the other numerous one, the thrush. Their nests were meticulously wood lined and their pale blue eggs, blotched tastefully with brown. Whenever we found a thrush's nest we both joined to admire it. "My, it's bonny," one or other of us always said.

Another nest builder we unreservedly admired was the wren. The best place to find their nests were on the upturned roots of fallen trees. The jungle of roots and soil seemed irresistible to wrens. We, more than once, found two nests on the same root. Each nest was a perfect little ball – slightly longer than wide – of woven grass and finished with a moss coating. A tine hole at the front did not allow us to see but a careful finger allowed us to feel and no harm done.

Robins were fond of the died down remains of last year's ferns and they only gave themselves away by a little hole in the fern debris – little but big enough for our sharp eyes to see.

In the woods and bushes there was always a smattering of finch and hedge sparrow nests to be found. Robins sometimes turned up in a bush too.

As a favoured spot for nests of all kinds, but particularly blackbirds and thrushes, the rhododendrons by the drive were challenged by the rocky railway cutting.

From the bridge, which let the road across which led to the farm, passing our door on the way, to the bridge, which carried the drive to the Big House, the railway ran through a cutting.

It was on the rocky sides of this cutting that we found lots of nests.

The birds seemed to have no problem that several times a day their nest was shaken by the clanking vibration, the whoosh of dispelled air and clouds of smoke and steam. They seemed, instead, to favour it for on each ledge of rock or clump of fern a nest was built.

Most common again were blackbirds and thrushes but robins and finches came there too.

And as an added bonus the wide shallow ditch beside the rail track, fed by the dripping walls, was full of newts. Move the dead leaves and there they were. We caught them, of course, but there was nothing much you could do with a newt so we just looked at them and put them back.

Though we dismissed the gulls as too easy we did score other ground nesters. "The crafty buggers," as Hamish called them.

Among the 'crafty buggers' were Mussel Peckers and ducks.

We were scouting the whins beside the Kyle – a prickly job but rewarding – when a duck flapped away at our feet. She had a broken wing and scurried across the grass in a panic, flapping helplessly and quacking. Show two boys a plump crippled duck and there can only be one outcome. We pursued with gusto and were finally dumbfounded when the broken winged bird calmly took off.

"Now there's a crafty bugger," I said to prove that Hamish was not the only one who could swear.

We could not find the right bush that the duck had come from under and therefore did not find her nest. But the next time a duck came out of a whin and flapped along with a broken wing we were not mugs and the nest was duly found and counted.

Mussel Peckers, which I have also heard called Oyster Catchers though they live on mussels and not oysters, were craft buggers too. They favour scraped nests on the stones beside the river. When someone approaches they rise with a din and fly away to a safe distance. Hunt as you may on the stones where the take off had taken place and there will be no nest. Get there quietly, though, the next time and watch the bird run maybe forty or fifty yards before taking off. Go to where that cunning run started and there will be the nest. Hamish and I were wise to that one.

Pewits nested in ploughed fields mainly. We often came across their nests when we were hoeing the turnips and carefully hoed around them. But if you set out across a newly sown cornfield you would never find the nest where the bird had taken off. She had adopted the Mussel Pecker's ruse and she added to it by swooping threats and alarm calls, which were increased rather than diminished as the intruder left the area of the nest. When he was far enough away to pose no threat to nest or young the alarm would be switched off and he would be left standing in the middle of the field looking a fool.

Mussel Peckers were not exclusive to the riverside. Some nested in the fields and others in more unexpected places. One pair set up home and raised their young on the side of the horse trough at the square. The daily visits of slurping horses did not offend them.

Another pair adopted the top of a strainer on the fence beside the road. It was an old post and had rotted in the top leaving a cosy Mussel Pecker size dip. The pair set up home and eggs were laid. They were unfazed by passing cars, vans and tractors but objected strongly and noisily to dogs and pedestrians.

I noticed that the female had a cord fastened round one of her legs and a trailing strand. I called in the assistance of Hamish and we devised a plan. It lives in my memory as one of the few plans, which I have devised, which has actually succeeded.

We borrowed a piece of string net from the stack-yard and while Hamish walked boldly up the field and got all the bird's attention I crept up the road, crawled the last bit below her line of sight and threw the net over the top of the post. The bird shrieked and flapped but I got her wings tucked into her sides and held her firmly, feeling the throbbing beat of her heart and avoiding the fierce stabs of the yellow beak. While I held her Hamish carefully unwound and unknotted what turned out to be fishing line.

When released, free of the line, our patient flew to the middle of the field and from there harangued us with every curse and insult known to Mussel Peckers. But she did not hold her grudge for long. As soon as we were heading back to the square she was back counting her eggs and then getting cosy on them.

Other ground nesting birds were stumbled across. Curlews, sand pipers and things like that but we could take no credit from finding them. It was pure luck.

The biggest and most obvious nests were those of the swans. There were lots around the Kyle shore but they were out of bounds. Parents told us horror stories about curious boys and dogs who had been done to death for getting too near swans eggs.

To Hamish and me such a ban was a challenge. And we decided to put our courage to the test. It was to be a pincer action. Hamish approached from one side and I from another. The one that the swan decided to chase would make a speedy exit and the other would make a quick run up. Look in the nest and be gone while number one was still fleeing. There was, however, a flaw in our plan. Had there been one swan it could conceivably have worked but we had overlooked that swans came in pairs.

When the pen rose from the nest, hissing, she copied Donnie and decided to chase me. I fled as if the devil himself was behind me but the swan was unwilling to go far from her nest and I realised that she was not pursuing me. I turned in time to see Hamish fleeing at speed from the cob.

When we met up Hamish stoutly claimed that he had looked in the nest and seen two eggs. I was dubious and argued the point.

"Well, we'll both count it," Hamish said and I knew then that he was fibbing.

"Liar," I said and the matter was closed and neither of us counted the swan's nest.

"We'll no bother with swans, eh?" Hamish said.

Although they did not count towards our tally seagulls were important to us. There were some stony places beside the river where they nested but they were seagull hamlets – on top of Invercarron Hill was Seagull City.

A long stretch of moor, peat hags, hummocks and pools stretched across the crest of the hill and on practically every hump and hummock there was a seagull nest. In each nest there would be one to five eggs, slightly smaller than a hen's and khaki, with black and brown – the original camouflage. We did find the occasional nest with more than four – nine in one case – but we assumed these to be shared accommodation.

The test to see if the eggs were worth taking home to eat was simple. Drop each egg in one of the ever-available pools – if it lay on its side on the bottom it was good, if it stood on end in the water it was dubious and if it floated it was no good. We did return the unusable eggs to nests but it was not an exact science and many a gull might have wondered why she suddenly had four eggs in the nest into which she had laid one. And there must have been a surge of confused parents with youngsters who held none of their quality genes, which they held dear.

The eggs were transferred home in knotted handkerchiefs. Sadly they were not always warmly received.

"I hope they've been checked."

"Everyone – they're all good."

They never were all good. But Mother knew that my assurance was worthless and broke each one into a cup before it went into the frying pan. I naturally enthused as I ate them and pronounced them delicious. The yolk was a bit redder than a hen's and even when cooked the egg was not quite opaque – rather like the consistency of melted candle wax.

The rest of the family were not so keen. Peter was all right – he would eat anything – and Father would try them to please me and lie to me that they were good. The females, however, lacked such tact and turned up their noses.

My Mother sometimes used the eggs in baking. They gave a faint pink shade to cakes and sponges but there was no drop in flavour or quality and even the women folk were won over on that.

Our preoccupation with birds was not entirely based on finding their nests.

One could not live in Invercarron with out being aware of the attention of birds. On the bright summer evenings when I was in bed long before sundown the open window allowed the creaking calls of corncrakes from the fields and the echoing calls of cuckoos from the woods. No birds were welcomed more warmly on their first arrival but we were all praying for them to shut up before the season was over.

We were excited to see a new bird at the turnip shed. My father made enquiries from some bird expert in Ardgay and we found that they were collared doves. The beautiful birds had not long ago come across the channel and now here they were with us. Unlike them were the famous magpies that did not venture further north than the Struie.

On a cold morning of snow we found our cotoneaster hedge crowded with colourful waxwings. They stayed for little over an hour but stripped every berry.

In the fields west of the steading there was a pond, which we called the Lochie. In early spring it was a place to witness a swarming mess of sexy frogs, later it was a possibility to find moorhens nesting there. Then I wandered in on a scene of massacre there. I arrived quietly and around the edge of the Lochie there were about a dozen herons scooping up the emerging froglets as fast as they could. I watched for a while but felt sorry for the frogs so stood up. The herons flew grudgingly off with croaking protest.

I stood for a while and probably saved a few hundred, maybe a few thousand frogs, but it was time for tea and I was hungry so I went home.

At about the same time as I was sitting down to my tea I suspect the herons were resettling to theirs.

SUMMER

Football was played all the year round but for me, in winter, it was a spectator sport. The Ardgay team played in a Poplars field beside the manse and upset the minister with their ripe language. These players were men and the matches were hard fought. Teams from all over Easter Ross comprised the league – Bonar was then a foreign land being in Sutherland – Alness, Balintore, and so on. They were hard places to go and play in – and doubly hard to get out of if you won. Poor Tom MacKenzie watched games with desperate interest – a win for Ardgay could mean a stoning for his bus.

In the summer football was more relaxed. It took place in the long bright evenings and varied in degree of importance according to the venue.

At the bottom level was the kick-about in Invercarron.

Someone, usually young Duncan or Jim, would take the football out into the little park beside the square and start belting it against the dike. The sound of the ball hitting stone attracted a steady flow of participants who had finished their tea, done their home work and been allowed out. At first the ball was passed around and kicked back and fore and then someone would realise that there were enough bodies available to make two five or six a side – four a side would do at a pinch – teams.

Then there was the humiliating picking of sides. The captains seldom varied – they were self appointed – if they were there then Duncan Junior and Jim did the picking and if one of them was missing it fell to Peter or Hamish's big brother Harry to stand in. The latter two were invariably the first choices. It was from there down that things got hurtful – not only was it desperate to have girls chosen before you it was equally hurtful to have someone younger selected first. The poor sod who was picked last – and it was quite often me – was ordered into goal.

"No!" I would protest. "I'm no good in goal."

"You'll be fine."

"I was in last night."

"And you were alright."

"I wasn't – I was hopeless."

"Go on, give it a go."

"I'm not staying in all the time," I would grudgingly admit defeat.

There was an upside to having no expectations resting on one's shoulders. When I reckoned it was about a quarter to seven I would wander off home and listen to "Dick Barton". It was sometimes a bit humiliating to come back and find that no one had noticed you had gone.

The ball was the usual hard leather cannon ball, which could knock a small goalkeeper into the goal with it. On a lovely dry evening the ball was vicious but when the pressure in the ball had sagged or it was wet the damage that could be done by it was multiplied tenfold.

A sensible goalkeeper, I would sidestep a hard shot and would rather put up with the derision of my team. This was balanced by the forwards who would sensibly ignore the captain's yells of "Head it!"

There was too a danger in concentration lapses. On each evening there were different teams and someone who was on your side on Tuesday would be on the opposition on Wednesday and a slip of memory which led me to pass the ball out to what I took to be a defender on my side but who shot the ball back past me into the goal – to the ridicule of my team-mates and the boisterous hilarity of my opponents.

Just when I was finding my feet in these kick-abouts Peter decided I could join him on a bigger stage. When these meetings were arranged I was not privy to but I would be shepherded off to Ardgay in the company of Jim, Harry, Peter and Hamish – no girls this time.

The pitch we used was the small field next to the Poplar's stackyard. It was narrow and long. Like the turnip shed at Invercarron the walls formed the sidelines and the dikes were an integral part of the pitch – a speedster could wallop the ball against the wall, race past a slower opponent and pick up the rebound without breaking stride. It made for fast and furious games. We even had the luxury of goal posts – not proper ones with a cross bar but fence posts driven into the turf. The rule was pretty much that if the ball went between the posts it was a goal – it could be threatening to go into orbit but it was still a goal. It was another case of the poor wee goalie being on a hiding to nothing.

Then we went even further afield. Up the hill behind Bonar to a field beside the Poor House at Migdale. It had the luxury of two proper goal posts complete with cross bars but it was not without perils. A line of whin bushes – a devil to get the ball out of or even worse to get shouldered into, marked the side of the pitch against the wood.

On the other side short heather encroached the playing area interspersed with areas of solid, grey rock. The combination made for some bizarre bounces.

There were the usual subjects from Ardgay there and added to them Bonar lads and more from round about. It was not a question of seeing if there were enough to make two sides – here we could get as many as fifteen a side and we hardly knew who was on what side. If they looked like they were going to try to get the ball off you you assumed that they were the opposition.

Players could be divided into levels. There were those like me who was keen enough to get the ball and run a bit forward and then try to pass it, all preferably without getting crunched in a tackle. There were the speedsters who usually flew down the wing with the ball stuck to their feet and then crossed, their job done. And there were a few who were terrorists. They took no prisoners, they chased the ball, deeply unhappy if they were not in the thick of all the action. One such was Charlie Forbes who was a stocky kid who put his head down and charged. His tackles were brutal – on the rocky escarpments he did sliding tackles which struck terror into cowards such as I and they were even more impressive when a stream of sparks flew off his calliper – he was a boy to be avoided but he was personally responsible for the quick reflexes of many boys in the district and maybe contributed to a few boys taking up the high jump.

When the football was over the cycle race began. We were poised on the top of the hill behind Bonar looking out over the Kyle to Ardgay with Carn Bhren behind and, slightly right, there was a map of the mouth of the Carron with Gledfield and Invercarron laid out. Our house was shyly hiding in the trees but the farm and the fields were open for inspection. Further right there was Carbisdale Castle backed by the mountains stretching away out West to where the sun was gradually sinking in a glory of red and gold.

We did not pause to take in the view. The race was on, thankfully down the steep hill first, over the bridge and on to Ardgay. Then the railway and through MacNamara's wood. It was cycled as if the hounds of hell were snapping at our back wheel but, like Formula 1 cars, we usually arrived at the finish in the same order as we started – once we left the road there was no prospect of overtaking so speed down the hill to Bonar and courage to go flat out across the main street onto the bridge was vital – he who hesitated at the crossing lost all the hill's momentum and was lost.

I know that it is turning recognised wisdom on its head but our efforts at cricket were more brutal than football.

The games were played on a field at the Goat Wife's croft on Ardgay Hill. It was a steep hillside and not ideal for any game.

Thankfully we did not have a proper hard ball but used a tennis ball instead. The batsman was a lonely soul – not having enough players for sides and everyone wanting to be involved at all times we all played against the batter. To accomplish a run he had to get to the bowling end and back – practically impossible. Fipperies like LBW and boundaries were not recognised. There were hot disputes about throwing rather than bowling and when, without the advantage of a marked crease, when a batsman was in. It was a game of continuous disputes.

We smaller fellows were picked out on the fringes and shouted at if the ball came our way. Bowling was the privilege reserved and fought for by the big boys. Sometimes, if there was time we'd get to go to the wicket and hold the big bat and be bowled out first ball.

Runs were scarce, ducks were plentiful. Most times a score of three would be enough to win the day. Peter once scored six – a record that he holds to this day.

A more leisurely evening could be spent at Kyle Cottage. There lived my friend and namesake Willie who was the son of the staunch Free Church hoer Hughie – but I did not hold that against Willie.

We had a variety of mutual enterprises.

In the wood behind Kyle Cottage the Two Willies (As Willie's mother called us) built a dam and diverted a stream. The soil in the wood was soft and after only a few days the stream had carved out a deep trench and as a result of out efforts arrived at the road a long way away from its original culvert. That probably puzzled the roadmen. It made us feel Godlike – we had altered the face of the land.

Another of our joint efforts was building a model world in a little quarry beside Willie's gate. The soil in it was pale clay and perfect for building roads and houses. Across the back of the quarry against the back wall we built tall houses – it looked like a pale Petra – and such was the tacky quality of the soil that it allowed our buildings to survive nearly all summer. Even the rain did not destroy our work – the smoother edges were blurred but actually made our buildings look older and more lived in. We approved nature's assistance.

I am puzzled why midges did not bother us. If I went into that sheltered nook now I would be the main course for thousands in a few moments. But memory of then has no place for midges.

The other task allotted to the Two Willies was to bring the cow in for milking. It was not really a job – all we had to do was to open the gate and the cow would make her leisurely way to the byre and stand in her stall ready to be milked.

There was, and I think is, a glass porch in front of Kyle Cottage and there we would sit and have a mug of still warm milk and look out across the Kyle to Balblair.

The field at the Poplars where we played football was also the site of the visits from Herchers with their Fun Fair, which we called The Side Shows – probably because at Highland Games that is what they were – a side show.

On a still night we could hear the music from Invercarron – there was no ignoring it. The usual form was to have a dry run to see what was what on a Wednesday or Thursday. The idea was to spend no money on that visit but it was hard so we would weaken and take along a couple of bob. The real time to go and take as much as we could scrounge was on Friday or Saturday evening. Then the young couples would come and excitement would be high – it was much cheaper to watch others spending than to do it oneself.

On our first inspection we would size up the various attractions and decide if any offered the prospect of financial reward. None ever did, but we never gave up hope. The rules were always stacked against us – a salutary lesson for life.

The shooting gallery was a sure fire twist – in an area where keepers were thick on the ground to have a fair shooting test would be a recipe for ruin and Hercher knew it.

It was guaranteed that no Friday or Saturday evening would pass without a dispute over guns.

"Look at it – the damn barrel's like a banana."

"You could shoot round a corner with this thing."

The darts stall was no better. There were guys straight up from the pub who could knock out treble twenties on demand who could not even hit the target card never mind get the arrow in the ace.

The kids behind the counters were unfazed by the abuse coming their way but there was a marker over which they would not allow anyone to cross, then the solution was simple – they yelled "Dad!" and a chap the size of a haystack wandered up and wondered sadly "What's the matter?"

There was a stall, which, if coconuts had been available, would have been a coconut shy. In the absence of the nuts a row of little pyramids of tins were laid along a shelf and the test was to knock them off. It seemed simple enough until you paid your sixpence and were handed three powder puff balls, which would not threaten a butterfly. To make doubly sure that there was not a run on the prizes the tins were filled with concrete.

There was a penny slide thing, a sloping wooden slot led through the mesh surround and the challenge was to roll your penny down and get it to land on a square beyond. It seemed simple enough until you read the small print – "No part of the penny could touch the line" – if you laid it down carefully with your hand it would have needed a steady hand to avoid a line. If the impossible did occur and you managed to avoid the line you could get three pence back – if you managed to do a corkscrew roll and the penny landed within the lines of a square at right angles to the launcher you could win a shilling but football pool odds were much more generous than those.

Hoop-la was another game of superhuman skill. The wooden

hoops were small, the prizes would appear to have been chosen for their irregular shapes and just in case that was not enough each prize was balanced on a wooden block. To win the prize the hoop had to pass all the way down to the base of the wooden block and lie flat on the table. I have seen prizes won but not often and usually by a tall, tall man who was then accused by the kid behind the stall of leaning over – a sin which necessitated its own sign.

There were two round abouts. The slow one turned gently loaded with pre-school passengers who waved nervously each time they passed their parents or screamed enthusiastically until a parent leapt forward and pulled them off. The seating arrangement on there was mostly wooden animals with a couple of double decker buses (marked "Highland") and a fire engine with a raucous bell.

The other roundabout was for daredevils like me. It flew round and heaved up and down at the same time. I did once make the mistake of choosing to sit on a motorcycle it was a wooden cut out and horrendously slippery – my hands and arms just lasted long enough to prevent me being flung to my death. After that I was choosier and found a pew with a side on it.

The ultimate ride was the swing boats. They were specifically designed for young men to show off in. The young women screamed and the man pulled on the rope so hard that the stays hit the top frame and the guy in charge started shouting and ran over to apply the brake – a long plank of wood which scraped along the bottom of the gondola when it passed at the lowest part of the swing – an exercise in betrayal which only made the young beaus try even harder.

I went on the swing boats, usually with either Peter or Hamish. There was no choice – not to go on would be to mark one for life as a wimp. Added to which when on the horrible contraption one had to pretend to pull vigorously on the rope and pretend to be enjoying it. Each time I reached the top of the swing my backside rose from the seat and for a dreadful moment I knew that I was going to plunge to my doom.

All the time there were throbbing lights and beating music, interspersed with shouting, screaming and laughter. It was warm evening summer magic – the long days past and the darkness drawing in. The sky still pale in the west but scattered with stars.

THE ELECTRIC

Old Duncan was not alone in his suspicion of the Electric – he thought electric was too near to fire for comfort. When we were, as a community, hooked up it was the biggest single step that any of us had experienced.

Dolly Campbell was alarmed by the perceived relationship between electric and fire too. When a neighbour visited and found her sitting in lamplight he asked if there was a power cut.

"No, no, it's on alright," she cast a glance at the light switch by the door. "I had it on earlier."

"Oh," the visitor was baffled.

"I don't keep it on all the time. Have you ever felt how hot the light gets?"

"The bulbs?"

"Aye, the glass bits. I touched it and it was red hot. Near burnt my finger. If it kept getting hotter and hotter it might just explode and there's no saying where that might lead. Fire, I wouldn't wonder. I am only sorry I ever let them put it in my house."

Efforts on the part of the visitor to reassure her came to nothing and for the rest of her life Dolly would put the electric on for a wee while in the dusk while she filled and lit the oil powered Tilley.

For everyone else the step into modern living was exciting and releasing.

At the farm complicated power systems operated by belt drives to tractors were replaced by motors – press a button and as many horsepower as was needed was instantly available.

Where evening jobs and night emergencies had been shadowy exercises carried out by the dim glow of lanterns, now there was instant overhead light. Admittedly not at first a very bright light, the bulbs favoured were not strong enough and the light cast was more an easing of darkness than a shedding of light. But in spite of Duncan's foreboding the electric was patently safer than oil filled lanterns put down in beds of straw. Farm fires were common, when the proximity of kicking cattle, straw and lanterns are taken into account it is a wonder that there was still a steading standing.

In the houses the change was a step into modernity. From a daily drudge ruled by paraffin, coal and wood we stepped into the twentieth century.

There seemed nothing which was not changed and it is difficult to know where to start.

The most obvious and noticeable change was the light.

An Aladdin lamp lighted our living room. Most folk relied on a Tilley. The Tilley had a fuel tank base, a slim upward rod to the mantle, which was inside a white glass globe. On the Aladdin there was a brass-fluted base leading up to the fuel tank and a tall clear, glass chimney at the base of which was an egg shaped mantle. Both were pressurised and gave off a welcome heat as well as light.

To go and do something in the scullery another lamp had to be lit – smaller than the Aladdin but similar in shape it was not pressurised and did not have a mantle.

For going off to bed we were given a "Ghostie". It was a very small lamp with a round tank base and a chubby white, round glass funnel with just a string-like wick inside. It did not penetrate the dark but gave enough clues to find the bed and certainly not enough to read by. The spooky shadows it cast were the reason we called it the "Ghostie". It was not a name which eased a childish superstitious mind.

The transformation of the arrival of the electric light was dramatic. Go to the scullery, the toilet, a bedroom and not have to have all the elaborate business with the lamps was a huge freedom. Every time such an expedition. When completed, was met with the same question. "Did you turn off the light?" one or other parent said it every time. To leave an unnecessary light on was a sin up there with murder.

The wireless had previously been battery operated. MacKay's Garage in Ardgay charged the batteries for a few pence a time. They were bulky acid jars, which weighed a ton. We had two such batteries on the basis that while one was in use the other was being charged by Hamish MacKay. For the most part Father had the unenviable task of cycling up and down the railway track with a battery in his post bag but it had from time to time fallen to one of the children – mostly Peter – to hump the thing. Happily for me the Electric came before I was in danger of being judged fit to be a battery coolie.

In spite of the apparently foolproof system we were often plunged into radio silence by a dead battery. "God know how much charge they put in that thing!" Mother would say and we all cursed poor Hamish MacKay – our curses were ineffective, Hamish lived well into his nineties.

Mostly these breakdowns were of a temporary nature until Father got home and swapped the batteries – my mother was convinced that this was a perilous job which could, if not carried out correctly, result in an explosion, flying acid and hideous disfigurement. Even when a recharged battery stood ready beside the dead one we had to leave the terminals untouched until Father came home. There were longer periods of deprivation. A battery, newly charged, gave up life and left us in limbo for near a week.

"You're not slaves to the wireless are you?" Mother would snort when we sighed because we were missing "Dick Barton" and "Paul Temple" and we knew full well that she was missing it too – it was on all day while we were in school.

Now the batteries were put carefully in the shed – they might be handy – and sat there for the next forty years. The battery-charging arm of MacKay's business collapsed and he put a penny on the pump to make up for it.

Ironing had been a complicated business involving a metal box iron and two heavy stone ingots. There were put in the fire and when red-hot one was lifted out with the poker – there was a fitted hole for the purpose – and slid into the iron. When it had cooled the changeover took place. The transfer of the red-hot billet was always a nerve shattering session with shrieks from mother interspersed with demands to "Stand well back" – we would've had to go into the garden to be further away.

The new electric iron was smart, sleek and clean. Both the girls suddenly found that they wanted to do some of their ironing. The boys were made of sterner stuff and farsighted enough to realise where such action might lead.

'The Range' occupied the major part of one wall of our living room. This was a black metal monster with polished silver trim. The mantle across the top was fully six feet from the floor and equally as wide. Across the top of the range there were two big metal cupboards, which supposedly were for warming plates but in fact were excellent clothes airing cupboards – pyjamas came out cosily warm. Below was a rack of bars for hanging things on. Then below were two big ovens and between them the fire. Everything centred round the range. It was our one source of heat and the one means of cooking.

My mother had an ambivalent relationship with the range, which swung from polishing pride to bitter criticism.

The ovens were always too hot or not hot enough. They did not heat evenly and if she opened halfway through a baking to turn the cake or sponge round the damn thing fell in the middle.

The top was not any better. The kettle was always there but when the broth and tatties and all the rest were on it was a dangerous clutter and took a lot of juggling and oaths to get everything moved around dodging the plumes of scalding steam. It was a minor miracle to get everything going at once.

"This damn thing'll be the death of me," Mother would say every day.

But she outlived it.

The electric brought a (small) cooker, which sat on a table in the scullery, and beside it was an electric kettle. There were four rings on the top and like the oven they were thermostatically controlled. Cakes came out even and uniformly risen and each pan had its own space and heat on the top.

It took a bit of getting used to but gradually the centre of activity moved from the range to the cooker. The last remnant on the range was the black kettle.

In some process between my parents and the landlords, (we and the farm were not part of Invercarron estate but, strangely, part of Gruinards which was miles away up Strathcarron – but lots of these big estates had land that stretched for miles) it was decided that the range could go and a plain fireplace be built in its place.

The job was given to local masons, James and John Ross, and they decided that they would come and start the job on Christmas morning.

To put that in context it should be said that at that time Christmas was not a holiday. My father worked as usual, shops were open and only the banks and the schools nodded in the direction of Christmas. For all else New Year was the holiday.

We were, however, as a family not unaware of the excitement of Christmas. Radio and newspapers had brought the awareness of what went on elsewhere. We four children hung up our stockings and, I for one, fully expected Santa Claus to come.

So Mother was not best pleased when she got wind of the proposed starting date.

"Christmas morning! They can't come then," she harangued the messenger who was father.

"If we put them off goodness knows when they'll come," he reasoned. "We've been waiting for months for them already."

Fortunately for my father Mother was well aware of the abilities of the Rosses for putting off and finally the argument collapsed and for Christmas morning the fire was lit in their bedroom and that became the proxy living room.

"It won't be for long," Mother said and repeated it daily until it began to sound like a prayer.

The removal of the range, however, was a big job. It was close to the removal of the whole wall and then the New Year came and work stopped for a few days.

When finally the new concrete surround was in place with a grate in the small space in the middle we were all delighted.

"It'll need to sit for a week – ten days to be on the safe side."

James sucked on his pipe as he stood in the drift of debris before the new fireplace. "If you put on a fire too soon, Missus, the whole thing might crack."

I think it was the only time I have witnessed my mother speechless.

There was a blitz of cleaning while the cement sullenly dried and finally one evening a little fire was lit and we all gathered to witness it.

"Not much heat off that," someone said.

"There's no coal on yet," Mother said cheerfully. "When we can get it properly banked up it will be as warm as toast in here."

"It'll never be warm in here again," one of the girls said sadly and in our hearts we all agreed.

But not for the first time in her life Mother was right. The new wee fire was gradually worked up to an inferno of sticks and coal and the whole room was warm – but we were loath to admit it.

"It's the lamp we're missing," Mother said. "It gave off such a grand heat."

TRIALS

The Sheepdog Trials were held year about in Invercarron and Creich. Hamish and I were always there early and made sure that Old Duncan was aware of our presence for we would get the summons to the committee tent and given the programmes to sell.

Most folk came early for the morning was given over to the locals. For the purists the afternoon open competition was the main event when handlers from all over Scotland came. But it was the locals who provided the fun and though most of the attention was focussed at the top of the field their fate could be sealed at the bottom.

To the casual observer it would appear that the local sheep-dog trials were as fair a test as could be devised for man and dog. The set up of the gates, the position of the pen and the award of points for each manoeuvre was the same for everyone. But there were variables and in charge of the variables was Watt with the help and connivance of his friends.

At the bottom end of the field, far from the scrutiny of competitors and audience, there was a large corral of sheep which it was Watt's responsibility to release in batches of five for each handler.

The sheep were local Invercarron beasts and to make up the numbers some were brought in for the occasion from Croick.

Experts in local geography will testify that it is difficult to find a flatter piece of land than Invercarron Farm, wedged as it is between the Kyle and the Carron. They will be hard pressed to name a hillier farm than Croick. The Invercarron sheep lived on the lushest grass, their poor relations from Croick nibbled the odd grass blade it could find among the heather.

The top speed of the fat Invercarron sheep was a sedate trot while the lanky Croick toughs could jump and run like the deer with which they competed for pasture.

The shepherd who Watt issued with five Invercarron animals only had himself or his dog to blame if the flock ambled past a gate instead of through it. By the time they reached the pen they would be so breathless that they would gladly enter in the belief that they might there have a rest.

The handler who was given Croick sheep had a more daunting task. The main problem was that the sheep could outrun all but the swiftest dog. When presented with the novelty of a flat surface their main aim seemed to be to head for the surrounding hills - they need not break their stride when confronted by a normal farm fence, they were, after all, used to deer fences. It was not unusual for such a group of hooligans to avoid all obstacles and demoralise the dog and humiliate the handler.

A crofter, and his trusty collie, would practise for weeks at home - practised with his few sheep who eventually realised that the quickest way to get back to peacefully chewing their cud was to trot through the gates, pop into the pen and not make any difficulties. To bring the resultant skill before his friends and neighbours was to be the high point of his year. But he - or maybe his father, years ago - had offended Watt and so that old devil gave him the sheep from hell. Could there be anything worse?

Well, actually, there could.

Watt was an old man and set in his ways. His dress of tweed never varied, his green stockings, which accessorised his plus fours, were always green and his tackety brown shoes always had upturned toes. He had been abroad during the First War but his tales were rarely of fighting - rather the opposite. He seemed to have spent a lot of time meeting the natives – mainly the female portion. He could tell us kids things about foreign women, which made our hair curl. Geordie had heard some of his reminiscences when we were at the hoe and had been rash enough to suggest that Watt was making it all up.

Watt just smiled, sucked his pipe and said, "Maybe, maybe!"

Geordie had not been a soldier – Watt referred to flat feet but that may not have been the whole story – and it seemed that Watt did not worry about his opinion. That was a mistaken assumption.

Geordie had probably forgotten the incident before the end of the day. Watt had not. He bided his time and now his time had come. Geordie strode confidently to the post, which marked the handler's position, and his sleek collie came so close in his wake that his nose might have been glued to Geordie's boot.

Five Invercarron ewes for Geordie? He had known Watt all of his life and must have thought he would surely oblige. But Watt bore a grudge. So five Croick stags, then? That would, indeed, be a crushing repost for a past slight. But Watt could do better than that.

Sheep from the same flock will generally stick together in a tight group. Different flocks offered no such allegiance. So when, through his telescope, Watt spied Geordie's walk to the post he had his assistants release three Croick sheep and two Invercarron ones.

When the groups were released at the bottom of the field they normally got their heads down for a bit of a snack while, unseen, the dog made a wide sweep to approach from behind and gently chivvy them towards and then through the various obstacles.

That was the usual and clearly the Invercarron ewes knew what was expected of them and began peacefully to graze. The others looked around and then fled doing jumps which would not have disgraced a springbok. When they met a strange, surprised dog they smartly about turned and fled towards the opposite horizon buffeting the peaceful grazers with the slipstream of their passing.

There were three options for Geordie. He could have called his dog to heel and retired with grace. He could have had his dog guide the two peaceful participants through the course - he would gain no points but it would have made a point. Or he could send his poor dog to try and retrieve the run-aways and return them to the starting point to rejoin the two who showed no inclination to go anywhere.

Sadly for Geordie he chose the third option and we all knew he was on a loser.

Geordie was a stubborn man. He was a loud man. And he had a short temper. Having set out on a course he stuck to it valiantly and as he sent his dog back and fore across the field chasing the three miscreants he got louder and louder and more and more heated.

There was a time limit for course completion but long before his time was up the whistle was blown - as Duncan afterwards quietly explained, 'To save the dog from exhaustion and Geordie from a heart attack'.

There was another crofter who fancied himself as an expert but he was not popular. He was a surly man when sober and when drunk, which he frequently was, he was aggressive. To him, justly or unjustly I do not know, had been attributed the introduction of myxomatosis to our local rabbits. The story was that he had brought an infected rabbit up from the south. With or without his help doubtless the nasty disease would have reached us eventually but his hastening of its arrival made him even more unpopular. Surprising really! One might expect an agricultural community to welcome the eradication of the rabbit pest but it was not so. Rabbit meat was popular and good and had the advantage that the plentiful supply was not guarded with the feudal ruthlessness of deer and salmon. The poisoning and destruction of the rabbits did not go down well.

It was assumed by all right minded viewers that Watt would send out the very liveliest of the Croick sheep and the most docile of the Invercarron ones for this man. Watt did not let us down.

There was a prize for the 'Most Noise' and until then it had been safely in Geordie's keeping but this fellow had just left the beer tent and when it came to temper and noise Geordie was by comparison a novice.

It was solely for the sake of the suffering dog that the whistle was blown, there was no mention of fear of a heart attack. Panting the collie caught up with his cursing master as he strode through the grinning crowd towards his car. Some wag had draped the corpse of a myxy rabbit across his car roof and he grasped it and threw it towards his tormentors with a string of curses. As his panting dog leapt into the car the oaf helped it in with a hefty kick.

We kids booed and hissed and the adults growled but we only got cursed at as the car door slammed and the car slewed across the grass and away.

That put a damper on the day. Our joke, for we all felt party to it, had gone wrong. We mourned for the dog so loyally attached to so vile a master. But his departure did open the door for Geordie to be awarded the Most Noise prize.

Hamish and I wandered the field harassing each new arrival for their six pence.

I do recall one Invercarron trials when it bucketed rain all day – we did not sell many of the soggy programmes that day. But there was another time when the trials were in the field right in front of our house. It was cooking hot and my mother put pails of water over the fence for the panting, tongue lolling dogs.

The programmes were simple lists of handler's names and the dog names. Hamish and I did an animal survey of dog names and there was never a surprise. Ben, Glen, Meg, Mist, Nell, Sweep and such appeared over and over and were repeated every year.

Late in the afternoon new arrivals faded and our programme sales dipped and we went to the Committee tent to return the few unsold sheets and empty our pockets which were full of money.

"Well done, boys," Old Duncan was a bit red in the face and we put that down to the bottle of whisky and the amber glasses on the table.

He gave us our five bob pay – one year he must have had an extra glass for he gave us a ten bob note each. We had high hopes of a repeat performance but the next year the pay had reverted to five bob. We did not complain. We would have done the job for nothing.

The days after the trials might have been an anti-climax but there was all the activity of dismantling the course and taking down the tents to keep us going. And even when that was done there was one more pleasure we could screw out of it - on our knees we searched the trodden grass, which had marked the bar in the beer tent. Mostly we only got coppers with an occasional sixpence but we did (sadly only once) find half a crown.

BOGAN BHUIE

I had arrived too late to meet two of my grandparents. My mother's mother had died before I was born and all I knew of her was a black and white photograph on the dresser in Proncy. The photographer had, unfortunately, posed her in front of a large round bush so that the final result was a picture of a woman very like Auntie Babs but with a big Affro hairstyle. I was never told the details of her death – such things were not often discussed with, or in front of, children and by the time I was old enough to wonder it seemed a morbid interest.

My father's father had also departed the scene before my entrance. In his case there was no photograph, only a selection op yarns to explain his demise. There was a story that he had died of pneumonia; another that a horse had kicked him; and a final version saying he had been killed by a tree that he was felling. The last one seemed the most acceptable to me when I was a boy, so it is the one I adopted.

That left my Granny on her own in Bogan Bhuie – the name means "Yellow Bog" and was an apt title. The house was stone with a corrugated iron roof. There was no running water and no electricity. Before the house was a grassy bank, a sweep of heather, in which lay the well and then a steep track down the hill to Whiteface. Behind the house the moor stretched away, speckled by cotton grass and yellow whins. No other habitation was in sight but at night, away to the East, the Tarbetness Lighthouse flashed on the horizon.

When we visited we got the bus from Ardgay to Whiteface Post Office and set off up the hill. Near the base of the hill Bogan croft was tucked in below the tree line, long, white walls topped with red corrugated iron. In Bogan lived Jim and Bessie and their two sons, Andrew and Rory.

If we were spotted coming up the road – and we always were – Bessie would be at the gate to ambush us. My mother would sigh but smile and shout, "Coo – ee, Bessie" as we approached.

Bessie worried our mother for she used an earthy vocabulary and Mother did not know that I regularly heard similar or worse at the square or in school.

"How's the boys?" Mother asked.

"The buggers!" Bessie rolled her eyes. "Andrew the wee bugger's knocked the back oot o' Edinburgh Castle."

It turned out not to be such a disaster as it at first appeared. The casualty was a picture of the Castle, which the villain Andrew had knocked off the wall.

"Damn me, pity me!" Bessie wrung her hands. "Them boys'll be the death o' me. The other bugger, Rory, was sent home from school for swearing. God alone knows where the little bugger picks it up."

"He'll grow out of it," Mother encouraged without great enthusiasm.

"Wish he would, " Bessie said sadly. " But the little bugger is the splitting image of Old Jake."

"His grandfather? I didn't know him."

"Oh, a horrible man he was. He could start a fight in an empty room and hadn't a good word to say about anybody. But do you know the old bugger got a hundred and two people at his funeral. Imagine, a hundred and two!"

"He must have been well respected," Mother suggested.

"Not him! There wasn't one at his funeral, family included, didn't hate the sight of him. Just imagine how many would have come if he had been a nice man."

"Well, we better be off, " Mother began to turn up the hill. "We have to be back down for the bus at five."

"I'll hang a boxie of eggs on the gate for you. Don't forget!"

"Oh, that's kind, Bessie," and we escaped.

"She's no afraid to speak ill of the dead," she sighed. "And I hope to goodness the eggs are better than the last ones she gave me – the hens all nest in the bushes and who knows how old they are when they find them. But she means well, the poor soul."

The road from Bogan to Bogan Bhuie was steep and rough. When it rained it became a stream – two streams to be precise and with each shower the twin tracks were deepened.

Behind Bessie's house the trees covered the hill and on the right, below us, was Acharry Farm. A little way up the hill there was, beside the road, a gap in the trees and a space of perfect green lawn. "The tinkers' camp," my mother told us. Used by the travelling folk for generations when the trees were planted the ones that filled the old campsite were cursed and to this day stayed clear.

At the top of the hill the road, such as it was, swung left and the trees moved too – over to our right and in the bare opening moor on the hill top to our left was Granny's house.

It was not like Bessie's. Bessie's house and steading were joined, long and low and white. The roof was painted bright red. This was a stone cube, grey and dark. The roof iron, if it had ever been painted, had flaked and faded and was now grey with big rusty blotches, like camouflage. Two small windows faced us as we approached. The door had been red and before that black. Now it was both for much of the red had flaked off and the black, now faded to grey, showed through. Along the length of the roof there were three tiny skylights. Before we reached the house there were three stone sheds beside the track. They had been, long ago, the steading. The roof at one end had blown off, landed upsides down on the bank and had stayed there ever since. Every shed was full of wood, even the roofless one.

It seems unfair for me to try to describe Granny. She had born and raised eight children, much of the time on her own, and sent them off into the world. When I came to know her it was for a fleeting moment: she was an old lady, set in her ways, many of them strange.

The house was full of clocks but rarely did any of them match. "I like the company," she said, meaning the tick. For the same reason she liked the wireless. In those days the BBC shut down at night. Granny was not much for sleeping and she had dozed off in her chair in between nursing the fire. She had forgotten to turn the wireless off when the station shut down. In the early hours – "What a fright I got!" – she awoke to the sound of "The Teddy bears Picnic". It was, Uncle Peter, seemed to know, the song played for Engineers to check reception and technical things which had to be done in the dead of night and which we did not understand. Henceforth "The Teddy Bears Picnic" was greeted by smiles all round as Granny's tune.

It was that experience which led one of her sons, again Peter probably, to show her how she could twiddle the knobs and still have music and talk after the BBC had shut down. That the talk was in Dutch or German bothered her not at all – she was bewitched that these people sat up late like her just to chat and keep her company.

Granny was invariably dressed in black. She was a widow so that was the way to dress. Her hair was white and pulled back in a bun. Her black dress, occasionally decorated with a sprinkle of jet, reached her ankles and when she went out she slipped on her matching black Wellingtons.

Another sign of a widow on Skibo was that every year she received a cheque from Andrew Carnegie's heirs. It was an impressive piece of card from the Chase Manhattan Bank in New York and it was handed round with awe. It was for ten dollars and was taken to the Bank of Scotland in Dornoch or Bonar to be cashed. Granny was annually disappointed that it did not equate to ten pounds.

When we visited my mother always took a bit of baking. Granny did not bake, she hardly cooked, and meal times were as haphazard as her sleeping hours.

I went alone with Father on his Sunday day off. Granny found out that I was off school for the next week and immediately had the idea that I should stay and holiday in Bogan Bhuie. My father was not keen – he probably knew that it would go down like a lead balloon with mother. I was not keen either – I knew it would be a week of water carrying and wood hewing but mainly I did not like going to the toilet in the bog.

But Granny was persistent and Father did not want to upset her and was as putty in her hands so I stayed.

My bed was on the landing, with a tiny skylight and a lumpy bed with plenty of blankets.

"But there's no sheets, Granny."

"Where do you think you are, boy? The Savoy?"

The water carrying was not a big chore. The well was behind a wood and corrugated iron cover. The door was a fairly recent innovation. It stemmed from Bessie reading in the paper that there were toilets in these passenger aeroplanes. "You can't be too careful," Bessie said. "Oh, I know it's nonsense," Granny chuckled, "But there are sheep and deer going about at night. It's better just to be sure."

Lift off the cover and the green interior of moss and ferns and little green frogs sloped up from a pool of water so clear as to be transparent. In Invercarron we were used to peaty water the colour of weak tea and so soft it burst into bubbles at a rumour of soap. There was a wee battered enamel pan for transferring the water into the shiny steel pails. I lingered on the job. It was warm and bumblebees hummed in the heather and the whins and dragon flies the size of Spitfires whizzed past. And when I paused a round face topped with black hair stared back at me with pale blue eyes.

"I thought you'd gone to Invercarron for the water," Granny said when I got back having emptied half of each pail into my boots.

"It's a slow job", I said.

"Ach away Lad," Granny laughed. "It's no job at all at this time of year. I've gone over the in the winter and needed a hatchet to get the pails filled. That's when it's hard work!"

Granny's life was ruled by water and fire and I found the latter to be the hardest work.

Our days were spent in pursuit of firewood.

"But the sheds are full," I protested.

"I don't want to be caught short," she replied. "I can do without most things but I can't do without my fire."

One of the sons had made her a cart. It was a bulky wooden body on a set of remarkably strong pram wheels. There was a base and two sides to the body and the lack of front and back was designed for it to carry logs. But logs had to be cut and then carried to a path, which the hurley could reach.

Granny set out with her hatchet and bushman saw and I followed on pulling the hurley. When we reached the wood I was given my orders.

"Get a few of them logs loaded and back to the house," the commanding officer ordered.

Meekly I obeyed, loading three or four long logs onto the hurley. Before I could set off Granny reappeared through the trees with a big bough balanced on her narrow shoulder.

"Still here," she said. " Here put this one on too – no good going with half a load."

The hurley ran fairly easily but it was the unwieldiness of the load which caused the difficulties. The tracks were devilishly uneven and my load top heavy so the thing was constantly trying to tip over.

I took three loads over before I saw Granny again.

"When are we having dinner?" I asked with no idea of the time but I did know that usual feeding time had come and gone.

"God, boy, you've no long finished your breakfast."

We'd had brose with evaporated milk -hours and hours ago.

"Get another load over and then we'll go back to the house."

I took a load over and went back with the hurley.

"Just a wee minute," Granny shouted from the cover of the trees. "Come and give me a hand."

She was collecting a pile of smaller sticks.

"Grand for kindling," she said. "I'll pick them up later."

There were piles of kindling right through the wood.

When we finally got back to the hurley she started loading it up.

"I thought we were going for dinner," I protested peevishly.

"We're no pulling an empty hurley back."

And we didn't and I felt she had conned me and her smile made me realise that she thought so too.

Dinner turned out to be a boiled egg and a slice of bread. When I pulled a face she gave me her egg too and just had bread.

"Have you got a worm, lad?" she asked.

And then it was back to the sticks. Sawing on the horsey, splitting and piling against the gable end.

"You have enough here for years," I ventured.

"I've got to get plenty in. You never know what's round the corner."

And then we had tea, Bread and jam and tea made with evaporated milk, which tasted yuch!

Thank God! Auntie Jessie came for a visit on Wednesday and brought a ginger cake. That cake kept me alive until Friday when

Mother turned up to take me home. She was cool with Granny and I thought she had been worried about me.

We were on the way down the hill to catch the bus when she came clean.

"Leaving you here in your school clothes!" she snorted. "Just look at your trousers."

When we got home though she did me a big tea.

"I was famished," I said, betraying Granny.

"She means well," she said. "She's forgotten what her own boys ate. She means well."

I was coddled for a week and Father was given the cool treatment for the same time and then we all got up one day and it was back to normal.

The story as told to me by my father was that Granny died sitting in her chair by the fire with a smile on her face and the wireless tuned to Hilversim. Mother rolled her eyes at that tale but I decided it was a nice way to go so I believed it.

When Granddad Proncy had died I was sent off to school on his funeral day.

I was taken to Granny's. There was a crowd of black dressed men on the green before the house and I sidled my way in. My father and his brothers were at the house door and all the women folk were inside.

On a trestle before the door they laid the coffin and a tall grey minister came out of the house and stood behind it.

"Oh, hell! It's the Free church man." Someone said.

"He's not had a congregation this big for years," some one else growled. "We'll be here all day."

The minister did go on a bit. He was inclined towards long slow prayers with thoughtful pauses and there was talk of being scythed down by death and that we were all in imminent danger of being reaped. I did not think it applied to me but I noticed a few of the old men around me shuffled their boots and looked uncomfortable.

It was my first experience of the psalms being led by a presenter. He was an old man with a thin voice who sang the psalm line by line and the gathering sang each line back to him.

"I to the hills will lift mine eyes." He sang and all the men around me imitated him,

"I to the hills will lift mine eyes."

It was slow, deep and moving. It felt like an echo of age-old worship on that hilltop in the soft rain – a rumbling of the faith of our forebears swelling from the land on which we stood.

"By cool Siloam's shady rill."

"By cool Siloam's shady rill/"

"How sweet the lily grows."

"How sweet the lily grows."

And then the sons lifted the coffin and as the women slipped back tearfully into the house Granny was borne away.

The hearse was too low slung to tackle the road up the hill so the coffin was carried all the way down to the main road. Past the sheds full of sticks and past the well.

At stages the cortege hesitated while the bearers moved up the line, the two at the head dropping back and two new ones coming in at the back.

Down past the green plot, which was the tinkers' site, and down past Bogan Croft.

At the gate stood Bessie. A black shawl over her head like a photo from St. Kilda. Her lips moved as if in silent prayer but Bessie was not praying, she was counting.

HEROES AND ZEROS

Like aunts I had a wealth of uncles. Four on one side and five on the other without adding in the ones who married into the clan.

On my mother's side there were three I did not know.

Willie, who died in his teens of a sickness which nowadays could have been mended by a pill, was revered as a near saint – the poor lad did not have a chance to be anything else in his short time – and to add insult to his memory I was given his name. It was my unfortunate lot to be compared – always, it seemed to me, when I was in my poorest light. That is why I have been left with the saintly image of the poor fellow.

There was Jim, he had gone to Canada before the war but he came back in a Canadian Army uniform and I was told that I can remember him. I can vaguely recall a lot of men in coarse khaki who appeared into our lives like spirits and as quickly disappeared. But which one was Jim?

I was shown a photograph and saw a broadfaced grinning stranger who lacked the hawk nose of all the other MacKays and 'Yes, of course, Mother, I remember him'.

He was the shortest of the MacKay boys but what he lacked in height he made up for in breadth. A man of immense strength. He was the one who shoved the foal aside and suckled the Clydesdale mare; he was the one who could toss a bag of oats up to the granary with one hand and without breaking a sweat. And he was the one who, when the war was over, went back to Canada to a place called La Prairie, which set us thinking of vast plains and faraway horizons – enough to make us, who lived in the crevices between the hills, feel a little dizzy.

And Donald. Ah! Donald! He it was who brought tears to the eyes and caused noses to run. I saw his picture too. A tall elegant man with a hawk nose above his sly smile, dressed in the gleaming uniform of the Seaforth Highlanders with a sergeants stripes upon his arm.

My father's sister Janet was married to another sergeant, Jack MacDonald, in the same regiment.

And both of these uncles were killed on the same day at El Alemain.

As a boy Donald had suffered from chilblains. With huge relish my mother repeated the story of how Donald, poor Donald, had been shoved out in the snow barefoot and told to run round the Proncy house. A run in the snow was, apparently, a well-known cure for chilblains. After a circuit Donald beat on the door. "Round again!" the torturers yelled. Three times they made him go round. "My how he howled, poor Donald," Mother looked far away to somewhere where I was not included. A world I did not know. "Did it cure the chilblains?"

"What?" She jerks back to the present. "Oh, I can't remember. I do hope so."

And both of these uncles were killed on the same day at El Alemain.

Kenneth was maybe the nearest my Mother came to admitting that the brothers were not all perfect. He was in the war too, "fighting for the bloody English according to the papers", he would say bitterly - but when he came home his marriage fell apart and Kenneth with it. He was over fond of the drink. He would turn up at odd times full of drink. My mother would fill him with broth and boiled mutton and give him pure hell and then spoil him with pudding and let him sleep it all off when he got maudlin and repeated, as he always did when he was tight, his belief that Sergeants Donald and Jack had been shot in the back by their own peevish men. Kenneth held that belief all his life. Where it came from goodness knows – maybe in some secret place in his own war experience he had seen such murder done. When he went he was warned carefully of the time of the bus he must catch but he usually made a little detour to Fergie's and buses were forgotten.

Late in his life Kenneth found his true love and courted her with love poems, which no one knew about until the new love died. But their love was never tested. Pulling down his case from the rack of a train in Biggar station on the way to a new job Kenneth had a heart attack and died.

Of all the brothers Alec was the favourite for I knew him best and longest. He was the youngest and I clearly remember him. Another soldier with a hackle in his cap. A commando we were told in a whisper – it was a special thing to be. And Alec survived the war though he was in many tight places, which he later smilingly shrugged off. He found a Welsh bride – who came, dear Mattie, and captured all our hearts. They settled in Criccieth and their home made an ideal, welcoming, holiday destination for many of their Scottish relations.

I had four uncles on my father's side, but though they were all in uniform they were not heroes, or at least no one said they were. My father did not talk about them or their exploits, so they remained vague shadows until they slipped out of the shadows and became real when I actually met them in later life - and even then they were not great talkers.

Peter was the one we saw most of. He was fond of his dram when he came home from working on lines of pylons and taking the electric to the remote corners. He was like my father an enthusiastic repairer of clocks but he, unlike my father, would have a try at mending watches. "I canna see the damn things," Father would say. Well into middle age in the remote corner of Raasay he meet his love and there he stayed for the rest of his life, being pampered and putting on weight and in the greatest comfort of his life.

There was a Donald too but I don't remember him. I remember the day he died. There was something on the Scottish news on the radio about a bank of a loch subsiding under a reversing lorry and the driver being drowned. "Poor man!" Mother sighed and when Father came home and told us the drowned man was Donald she wept.

Donald's son was to be my closest friend in my teens and we met again and rejoiced in the meeting when our paths crossed in the RAF.

And there was a Davey on that side too. He, like all his brothers, spent his youth taking apart and reassembling motorbikes and he alone put that knowledge to use when the war was done. He married into Aberdeenshire and turned his hand to bicycle and motorbike repairs, and expanded into blacksmithing. He was looked upon by us all as a success and though we laughed at his wife and son's accents we were secretly jealous when they left in a shiny motor.

And then my Father got a postcard. He would have been handed it in the sorting office. He handed it to mother without comment. It was a picture of the "Canberra" and the message was brief,

"Dear Brother, We are on our way to settle in Australia. We are just now passing Gibraltar. I will be in touch when we are settled. Your Brother Davey, Rosie and Alec."

Mother squawked in horror. Father made no remark though he must have been deeply hurt. We never again heard from Davey, he Rosie and Alec might as well have been dead.

There were cousins on my mother's side too.
One was a Mammy's boy who lived with his widowed mother and it was no surprise that she spoiled him for she had no one else.

What a strain it must have been for both mother and son when he was called into the Army. But my mother showed no sympathy for a situation, which I now find, pulls at the heartstrings. She was used to the men in her life taking off to war.

In the midst of the Sahara Desert Andy got out of their troop transport and spotted a man leaning nonchalantly on a nearby palm tree. It was Danny. Danny's home was within a mile of Andy's on the hill behind Bonar. But Danny was renowned as a man of few words. When Andy rushed up to him in the desert Danny's hands stayed firmly in his pockets and he gave a slight nod of the head and issued his standard greeting; "Aye, Aye". They could, as far as he was concerned, have met on Bonar Brae.

It was Danny again who was beside Andy as they carefully picked their way across a desert minefield. "What," wailed poor Andy," What would my Mam say if she could see me now?"

""Look where you're putting your bloody feet or she'll never see you again" was Danny's reply – which must rank as one of the longest speeches he ever made.

Mother would report these tales with relish and we would soak them up. We never wondered how she could know of these things.

It was an age of heroes. Unlike today however, when the title 'hero' has been devalued to mean anyone in uniform, these were mostly conscripted men. Dragged away from wives and families and for months, years sometimes, totally without contact. Maybe a letter every few weeks but no certainty on that. And their families did not even know where in the world they were. Had one of them complained to Mummy that his boots hurt he would have been in the glasshouse before his sore feet could touch the ground.

For a boy my age they were all heroes until proved different. And of course I'd learn that to be adult did not necessarily mean brave.

My first lesson came from the unexpected person of John Thain.

He was the gardener for the Big House and lived in a house, which was incorporated into the wall of the huge garden. He had endeared himself to my mother by writing to her in Proncy when Donald was killed. It was a tasteful, sincere letter and was treasured by her for the rest of her life.

It was shortly after we returned to Invercarron that we went to a bonfire organised by Thain. I am uncertain about details. I remember rain, lemonade, a huge bonfire and a figure of straw at the top of the pile. Whether that was Fawkes or Hitler I did not know or care but there was a cheer when he caught alight so I think it must have been Hitler.

Thain and his wife had been left in the gardener's cottage for the duration of the war while the Army occupied the Big House. Whether he was on the Army payroll I do not know but he kept the garden and the immediate surroundings of the house in order. He was marking time to peace. Maybe that's what his bonfire was for!

The garden was large and had a tall stone wall all round. Hamish and I were later to prove that it was not an effective barrier but at that time I was small and not yet criminally inclined.

The East wall of the garden practically lay along the riverbank; there was a path and trees between. An arched gate door was built into the wall. Opposite that door there was one of our favourite playgrounds – the river had cast up a big bank of sand. It was perfect for canals, castles, roads and houses and had the advantage of having no ravaging tides – what we built today would still be there tomorrow.

In Summer, which was the time we occupied the spot, the river was listless and gentle. The water was warm and soft on our toes when we paddled. It was probably as near to paradise as we would get.

And then one afternoon as we listlessly dug in the warm sand, the door in the garden wall creaked open and Thain ushered out a small, dark woman. He saw us and his face contorted with anger. "Away with you! Go on, away!" We all stood up and gawped at him in silence.

"No, no, it's alright," the woman said in an American accent.

"I'll not have it," Thain began to advance on us and we took to our heels.

Jean was hiccupping with anger when she related the event to Mother. She flinched and gasped. "The two faced…."

Father was hardly in the door when he was told in a five voice chorus.

"Ach, the poor man would be showing a buyer round," Father said. "He would have been under a lot of strain. Don't let it bother you."

"But it does bother us," Mother was not to be so easily swayed.

"He's probably regretting it already. Just ignore it. Don't start a feud with a neighbour."

And we did not. Thain was spoken to when there was no option but he would have been aware that there was no warmth in our "hellos". Mother went down 'to see Mrs Thain'. It was not mentioned as far as I know.

The woman on the riverbank was a buyer. She later showed herself as Lady MacNamara.

Thain retired and was replaced by a man called Bratchie.

The Thains moved to Dingwall. Mother went, maybe a couple of time a year to visit. "To see Mrs Thain" she would emphasise when we scowled. Sometimes one of us – usually me – was invited to join her on the visit. I would hang back and she would say, "Mrs Thain would like to see you." When she put it like that I would reluctantly agree – one would have been mad to turn down a jaunt on a train, a fancy tea from Mrs Thain and a look round the big shops of Dingwall.

And then the circus came to Bonar. My mother took Barbara and me to the matinee performance - not a popular decision, we thought the matinee was for wimps and most of our school friends were going to the evening performance. Even Jean and Peter were being allowed to go in the evening with their friends. "Not fair," we said but we were over-ruled.

Before we went into the big top we went into a tent grandly signed "menagerie". It turned out to be mainly the circus animals, ponies, a camel; a zebra, a cage of lions and a small cage with a large sign "Giant Rat". I knew the miserable occupant from the Encyclopaedia. "It's a coypu," I said. "Hush," said Mother and nodded to the attendant taking the money. He had heard me and he was staring at us and there was no doubt that he was not keen to join my fan club.

There were galloping horses and people swinging, but what we enjoyed most were the clowns. There was a business with a wee car which disintegrated much to our amusement. There was a session with a lot of water flying about and near the end one of their number began to sing a song.

Each verse of the song was announced and it went like this;

"Verse One,
"I was strolling in the park one evening,
"I was strolling in the park."

"Verse Two,
"I was strolling in the park one evening
"I was strolling in the park. "

"Verse three,
"I was...."
But you can see where this is going!

While this boring recital was taking place the other clown had retreated and came back with a cane with which he whacked the singer's bottom. When this failed to stop him he retreated again and came back with a stouter stick and repeated the dose. This escalation of violence went on to about verse fifty by which time the assaults were being applied with a huge plank. Being fitted with a clapperboard this made a very satisfying sound and all we kids, and most of the adults, were thoroughly enjoying it. Strangely I don't recall what the punch line was. Maybe there wasn't one!

While this had been going on the lions' cage was being erected in the ring. What I realise now and did not know then was that by placing the lion act at the end of the matinee and at the start of the evening show the circus staff only had to erect the cage once to accommodate both shows.

I cannot honestly recall much about the lion act. There was doubtlessly a lot of whip cracking and roaring

It was when the show was over and grown-ups were gathering their coats and their children that the excitement really kicked in.

One of the lionesses had slipped through the tunnel, which led from the cage in the circus ring to, presumably, the lion's cage outside the tent. Now she was wandering nervously under our tiered seats.

Several hard looking men, some of them carrying guns, rushed into the ring and one of them was shouting to the departing audience to stay still. The lioness was not an impressive sight as we looked down on her slinking under our feet; she was a thin mangy looking thing. But that was obviously not a shared opinion. While we stood obediently beside Mother several other members of the audience started a stampede towards the exits shouting and pushing.

Mother tutted and I looked on in horror. There were all those much respected, brave grown-ups. The lioness decided after a leisurely circuit that she might as well go home for her tea.

Back at school the matinee kids were kings of the walk, wimps we were not and the jealous attendees of the uneventful evening performance sought out our company and asked for repeated detailed accounts of the Great Lion Escape. The story was repeated and embroidered and perhaps there lies the start of my creation of fiction.

The grown ups, crofters, shepherds, everyday decent men never knew with what scorn I viewed them from that day on. They were my introduction to cowardice but they did not know it.

It was a long time ago. I forgive them now which does not do them much good for they are all long dead. So far as I know none of them met their end by attack from a man-eating lion.

SEORAS

I would need extra fingers to tally all the advantages of being the youngest of the brood – and the further behind the others the better!

One great boon was that my eldest sister Jean married while I was still in short trousers.

She married a policeman and they were posted to Melvich on the north coast – his own childhood stamping ground, which could have been awkward.

To me it offered a holiday destination beside the sea and foreign from Invercarron in many, many ways.

I just had to step off Burr's Post Bus to be aware that I was on foreign territory. There was the roar of the sea and tang of salt but overriding even the salt was the scent of peat smoke.

By some prior arrangement Jean had lined up a distant relative of her husband to take me under his wing. Seoras had spent his life at sea but was now living with his sister Bell in one of a row of cottages, which clung, to the cliff top in Port Skerra, which was – say it quietly lest they hear! – A continuation of Melvich, which spread itself, down the hill and ceased when it reached the cliffs.

Seoras was tall and thin, slow talking and, like Bell, happier and more at home in Gaelic. He worked at the mouth of the River Hallidale as a salmon fisher, which was akin to being a Santa Claus. No, not quite the same, the fishers did work hard for four or five months a year. Sometimes the money was good. I recall the ripple of excitement which circulated Bonar when the news got out that the boys there were on more than twenty pounds a week.

Salmon fishing took place all around the coast. In the shore side of the open sea, on the known highways of the salmon heading in for their own particular river, bag nets were hung in the water. Long reducing tunnels of net with traps which sent the fish ever further until they reached the dead end – the bag. These bag ends were winched onto the boats and the silver harvest spewed forth.

On the stations at Bonar it was hard work. The job moved with the tide so nights were fished as well as days but it was rarely fully dark in the summer but with a night of rain and black cloud it could be tricky enough.

On these Kyle stations the boats rowed out across the current paying out a net, then circled back to base and the net was winched in.

Sometimes there were salmon, sometimes there were not. Then as that net was repiled ready for the next shot onto the back of one of the boats another did the circuit and again the net was pulled ashore. This was hard work and offered no respite. I can remember four such stations operating on the Kyle.

By comparison the fishing station at Melvich was a holiday camp. They fished the lowest deep pool of the River Halidale. The river slunk into the sea at the end of the white beach and on its other side reared the black cliffs. The mouth of the river was permanently lost in the rollers coming in but the salmon could find it. Here, they fished by day; the tide did not affect the depth of their pool. One man sat on the cliff top and only when he saw salmon entering the pool did he shout and the boat was launched to circle the arrivals in the net.

The men had to be fast – the salmon were just passing through so did not linger. It was strictly against the landlord's rules – for it was he who rented out the fishing station – for stones to be thrown to turn the fish back into the net. The more fish that got past the nets the more there were for he and his cronies to catch by rod further up.

Throwing stones into the river was a job within my capabilities so I did it with vigour when I was down there.

I did not go down to the river every day but happened to be in attendance when the boss strutted along the riverbank. Nobody needed to tell me that he was the boss. The walk was arrogant, the plus fours were preposterous and the fore and aft hat was ridiculous.

"Beautiful morning, Cheps!" He was shouting as he approached. "Plenty of fish?"

"A few, a few," foreman Ken, replied. "We canna get them all."

"I hope not indeed," he beamed. "I hope there is no stone throwing. One of my guests thought he heard a lot of splashing yesterday."

"Ach he would be hearing the oars likely," Ken assured. "There's no one on my crew throwing stones."

"Glad to hear it. One of the lads at Bettyhill was sacked for it last week. It's not sporting, y'know."

"No worries for you here," Ken smiled.

"Who have we here, eh?" The boss had spotted me lurking in the background, half hidden by the boat.

"That's our mascot," Ken laughed. "He's here on holiday."

"Jolly nice place to holiday. I wouldn't change it for anything. I'm off up to see if I can get one of the blighters that you missed."

"Thalla mach! Thalla dhachaidh a' bhugair!" said Ken.

"Eh?" The wee man turned back. "Oh! The Garlic, is it? What did you say?"

"I wished you tight lines, your Lordship," said Ken smiling.

"Jolly kind! What a generous sentiment," and he turned away and set off back up the river bank.

"Tight lines, your lordship!" one of the men said softly and they all smiled.

I smelt a rat and looked questioningly at Seoras but he just grinned and winked.

I returned to the top of the pool ready to imitate the casual, bored boy who throws stones in the river.

Not every day was spent on the river. Thank goodness I had missed the peat cutting, which involved several jobs from Hell, but there was still work available. The peats lay flat on the heather and moss and were crisp and dry on top but still sloppy and wet below. The job was to pick them up and lean them together standing up so that the wind and the sun could get to the wet side. Sadly the already dry side had the consistency of iron and the texture of sandpaper and the other was gooey black. It was hard on the hands and hard on the back. And because it was a traditional sort of job my torturing brother-in-law thought it appropriate to supply traditional peat cutting refreshments – cold tea, yuk! And cold water and oatmeal, yuk! Yuk! Yuk!

On other days I walked with Jean across the brow of Scotland to Strathy for her to pay her duty visits to her in-laws.

It was a fair step, maybe three miles each way, but on a bonny day it was a treat. Beside and below us the sea grinding against the cliffs and the Orkneys floating, light blue, on the horizon. On the other side moor stretched away and before us, on the outward trip, the glorious shape of Ben Loyal.

We would stop at the MacLeod's shop at Baligill and enter the dark interior. It was packed with goods. Amongst things I remember were,

Sweets, spades, nails, candles, barbed wire, tea, snuff, butter, fags, fence posts, cheese, rat traps, tins of beans, binder twine, pencils, tins of peaches, writing pads, batteries, lanterns, pen nibs, paraffin, laces (shoe and boot), ink, oatmeal, dog biscuits, walking sticks, stamps, mouse traps, eggs, razor blades, bacon, tins of paint, envelopes, matches, bread, cat food, carrots, kindling, pans, scrubbing brushes, flour, soap, boot polish (black and brown), toilet rolls, potatoes, bottles of pop, pins and needles, pipe tobacco, salt, jam, tooth paste, dog collars, postal orders, biscuits, white puddings, hair grips, hammers, buttons, petrol, fish hooks, chewing gum, safety pins, sausages, hose pipes, hat pins, scissors, coal, dog whistles, treacle, Thermos flasks, baking powder, peat cutters, insoles and yesterday's papers. It was their boast that if they did not have what you wanted they would get it in.

It was the evening, though, that I looked forward to. I walked down the slope through Post Skerra with the cliffs of Hoy clearly visible in the evening sun and the corncrakes setting up their chorus in the fields stretching down to the sea.

At Shorus and Bell's I would be ushered in like Royalty. It was an old cottage, the floor was made of flagstones and a bit uneven and the windows were tiny so that even then, in the high summer, it was dim.

Seoras took me fishing off the rocks. Armed with long bamboo rods we clambered down the rocks and stationed ourselves just above the highest wave height and trailed our white-feathered hooks through the water. The waves swelled and sank smoothly and mightily and most of the time I could watch my row of white feathers skimming along just under the glassy surface. And sometimes I saw the fish swoop up and sometimes it was just my hands that received the signals but either way there was a rush of excitement. We caught lots of cuddies (cole fish), sometimes a mackerel or two, but Seoras said you really had to be out in a boat for them, and on one occasion a mighty blung (rock cod).

Cuddies and mackerel were scorned by the locals as scavengers and not fit to eat. I took a few to Jean and she fried them for me and I declared myself delighted by their taste – in fact the cuddies were bland and the mackerel oily. The remainder of our catch we took down to the beach and put in the/ stinking barrel for the lobster fishermen to use as bait in their creels.

On other evenings we went out to join the men on the cliff top. Every evening there was a group sitting on a bench above the bay. It there was too many for the bench, and there usually was, some sat on the short grass and some just stood. They talked softly in Gaelic as they puffed on pipes or sucked on cigarettes.

When Seoras brought me to the group he introduced me as Andy, the policeman's brother-in-law, "and he doesn't have the Gaelic."

They all looked at me sadly as if I was missing an arm or a leg but from then on as a courtesy to me, a mere boy, these old men spoke in English so that I was included.

When one of them forgot Seoras would gently cough and point at me. "The boy," he would remind and the speaker would stop, "I'm sorry, lad."

The talk was unhurried and disjointed. They touched on many topics and sometimes pulled me into them.

"I liked maths at school," Ian, a grey haired man in a blue boiler suit said to me. "Are you good at school, lad? What's your favourite subject?"

"I like English," I replied.

""Likely you'll be good at it," Seoras suggested.

"No bad," I agreed.

"You would be a scholar at everything likely," Ian was addressing Murdo and elderly man in black trousers and red, polo necked jersey with holes at the elbows.

"I was useless at science," Murdo admitted. "Bob was top every time in science and I was bottom."

"No quite bottom, I think," Bob laughed.

"You were in school together?" I asked.

"Aye, we went to Melvich School and then to Thurso together. It's a few years ago now mind," Bob laughed, he had a round red face and a white, short beard and he always seemed to be cheerful.

Below us a basking shark was cruising over the white sand in the bay bottom and we all paused to watch its leisurely progress.

"What a beast!" someone said.

"Aye, he's a big fellow," Bob agreed.

We had a grandstand view of everything that passed on or in the water of the Pentland Firth from boats and ships to whales and dolphins.

"Are you a MacKay?" Bob asked me.

"No, I'm MacKenzie."

Again that look that suggested that I was missing an arm or a leg so I hastily added. "My middle name is MacKay. My Mother is a MacKay and Jean's married to one."

"Ach indeed! You are well connected," Murdo laughed. "Nearly all this lot," he looked around him, "are MacKays. No, there's Archie – he's a Ross."

"Aye, from Lairg," Archie admitted. "No far from your own spot. My wife is a Port Skerra Mackay, though."

"She was working in the Sutherland Arms in Lairg when Archie got his eye on her."

So it appeared that only Archie and I were not MacKays. I was amazed that all these old fellows were still in the place of their birth and later that evening, when I was sitting at the table in their house with Bell dispensing tea and placing a whole salmon in front of me and putting a fork in my hand, "Help yourself just," she said, I brought up my question.

"Lord bless me!" Seoras laughed heartily when I remarked on the stay at home tendencies of his friends. "Now, Murdo, is like yourself, he's only .here for the holidays. He's a professor in some university in California. He comes back every year for a few weeks with his sister, she still lives in his old family home."

I tried to visualise Murdo in his red tattered polo jersey in front of a class of Californian students and failed.

"Bob was right through the two wars in the Navy – sunk God

knows how many times. But he's just retired from Cunard – he was captain on some of the biggest liners in the world."

"And then Bibba, as we call him, the big man with the bald head, he was a high up in the British Embassy in either Australia or New Zealand – I can't remember which."

"Oh!" I was impressed.

"And Tommy was some sort of top civil servant in London. Bobby, the wee fellow, he was a headmaster in Glasgow and Colin was headman in a bank in Edinburgh. Ian was a chief inspector in Glasgow Police."

"A lot of powerful men," Bell commented. "But all nice."

"You don't get to the top like they did by being nice," Seoras commented.

"That's an awful thing to say," Bell cried. "Now you just dig in – a bit of salmon is good for you."

The next time I met Murdo I looked at him in a new light but still could not see a professor hiding under his tatty red jumper.

"The very man," he said when we met in the shop. "I am going out with Bob in his boat this afternoon – do you want to come? They say there are a lot of mackerel about."

"Oh, yes please," I said then thought of peats. "I'll need to check with Jean."

"Fine, we'll see you down at the shore about two. Tell Jean you are going with Captain Bob and she'll know you'll be safe enough."

"Captain Bob," Jean said when I asked.

"Yes, Bob," I said to underline my position of being on first name terms. "And Murdo."

"You should be alright with them, " Jean laughed. "Did you know that Bob was a sea captain?"

"Yes, Seoras told me."

"You should see his house. His wife, Mary, has photos on all the walls of him with all his top passengers – Royalty, Presidents, goodness knows who else. Everybody who was anybody is pictured with Bob all over his walls. It must be a nightmare to dust."

And still, like Murdo, I could not visualise Bob, heavy with gold braid, shaking the hands of Kings and Presidents.

As on the cliff top my two companions spoke only English when we went out in Bob's very smart boat – it had a built in motor, most of the Port Skerra ones only had oars.

The sea was smooth with a mountainous swell and we hit a shoal of mackerel almost as soon as Bob turned off the engine and we cast our lines.

It was later, when we were having some of the tea, which Bob had brought in a flask, and chewing on biscuits supplied by Murdo, that I broached a subject, which had been niggling at my mind for a few days.

"Can I ask you something?"

"Ask away," said Bob.

"As long as it's not about sex," Murdo chuckled and I blushed.

"Can you tell me what 'Halla mach! Halla gachee u'voogair!' means?"

"'Thalla mach, thalla dhachaidh a'bhugair? Who on earth said that to you?" Murdo asked.

"Oh, it wasn't said to me."

"Who to then?"

"I was down at the salmon fishing and Ken said it to the wee Lord mannie."

Both my companions roared with laughter and a seal who had popped up beside the boat to look at us was startled by the sudden noise and dived.

"And did you ask Ken what it meant?"

"No, I didn't but the Lord mannie did and Ken said he was wishing him good fishing."

"The rascal," Murdo was still laughing. "Now, you see and keep this to yourself or Ken might be in trouble. He wasn't as you suspect wishing him good fishing. It translates roughly as 'Away with you, you wee bugger!'"

"Oh, " I said and joined in the laughter.

When I was due to go home to Invercarron, on my last visit to the fishers, there was a lot of whispered Gaelic chat between Ken and Seoras. I thought it unusual for them to break the speak English in my hearing rule.

It was on the way up the hill at the end of the shift as I walked proudly beside Seoras that he told me that Ken had been keen to give me a fish to take home but was not sure how it would be received in the Police House.

"Jean wouldn't mind," I said.

"No, no Jean wouldn't say anything but we thought it best not to chance it. It wouldn't be fair to put Jean in an awkward spot like that."

"Oh," I said, disappointed.

As I was about to clamber onto Burr's bus at the Post Office the next day Gordie, the youngest lad at the Salmon Station appeared at my side and thrust a heavy bag into my hand, "From Ken," he whispered and was gone.

Mission accomplished without embarrassing my hosts.

Jean's husband was moved from Melvich and I lost touch with Seoras and Bell. I was away soon myself and by the time I came back there were Smiths and Joneses and all kinds of foreign names in Melvich and Post Skerra.

Only recently did I visit the Strathy Cemetery to pause at Jean's grave in the beautiful place above the beach and the crashing waves. I walked round the paths. Here, at least, nearly every name was MacKay. I did not find Seoras or Bell and only afterwards realised that they might well be memorialised as George and Isobell.

I did see Captain Bob and his Mary and it did not matter that I did not find the others. I had no need of carved names to remember them.

SHEEP

When, in the church, in the autumn, the Harvest Thanksgiving service took place the church was full of fruit and flowers and sheaves of corn and bags of potatoes and turnips with huge cabbages and swollen cauliflowers. But there was no place or mention of the biggest harvest in the Highlands – sheep.

There was then, and probably is now, no croft or farm without sheep. The same sheep as were cursed and blamed for the land clearances, when homesteaders were forcibly removed to allow the landlords more room for sheep, were and are the major cash crop of Highland Agriculture. The feelings in the Highlands run high to this day on the subject of 'The Clearances'. There was, of course, unnecessary force used but that is ever the way of things when unseeing generals hand power to mindless minions. But, I may be treading on dangerous ground here, I am not convinced that the cleared crofters were in the long term badly done by. I have looked at the hovels where families lived with, and in no better circumstances than, their animals in the middle of desolate moors on patches of grass broken in by back-breaking labour and I wonder if it was such a bad thing to be sent to settle in countries where land and opportunity were available. There are many folk in America and elsewhere living today in comfort that must bless the day that their forebears were chased out of the bogs.

Other evicted clung to the coast. Bettyhill was a settlement established for some of these displaced crofters and was named after Elizabeth, wife of the Duke of Sutherland, the chief evictor.

Such thoughts did not affect me when I was a boy in Invercarron. There was talk of evictions and some old folk spat when the name of the Duke of Sutherland was mentioned, but it all meant nothing to me then. Sheep, however, meant a lot. To a great extent the sheep marked the progress of the year. At virtually every season the sheep had some sort of call upon farm time.

Like the first snowdrop and the first primrose the first lambs were welcomed with smiles all round. They usually started to arrive while I was at school but thankfully they continued to make appearances on Saturdays and Sundays and I was out there with the shepherd.

In Invercarron the sheep were Cheviots, big animals with, when pregnant, backs as wide as tables. They were normally docile but when their lambs were born they could be aggressive. I have seen the collie take a toss when he was silly enough to take his eye off a new mother. I was doubly careful – a stamped foot threat was enough to get me to move on.

There were around two hundred ewes on the farm, maybe half a dozen of them were black, like grains of pepper in a salt pot. They got an unfair share of attention from the children. What we wanted from a black ewe was a black lamb – they were just so much more beautiful – but from time to time we were disappointed when a white lamb appeared. One black ewe had twins and confused the issue by having one white and one black offspring. Another white ewe had a gene throwback and produced two black lambs.

There were no restrictions on the children. We watched each birth with close attention and when difficulties arose we were in the front stalls as we sat on the ewe to keep her still while the shepherd's hand and arm disappeared to turn a head or straighten a leg. The education was total.

Always hand in hand with birth is death. It was rare that a ewe died but lambs were very vulnerable.

The risks of birth in what was usually a cold, wet field were high enough but there were also vicious pirates on patrol, their minds set on murder. For us foxes were not a threat but some of the hill farms round about suffered from them. Ours was an aerial threat. Hoodie crows and ravens were always on the lookout for the weak and vulnerable but the giant black backed gulls were quite capable of attacking a healthy new born. It was a sorry education to come across lambs torn to pieces by these vicious birds or, in some ways worse, to find a still living lamb with an eye, or both eyes, missing.

There were a lot of big, fit ewes that produced just a single lamb. They were a disappointment. And then the younger, first time mothers, least fitted for the task, would go and have twins or even triplets. Triplets were not popular – after all the ewes were equipped to feed a maximum of two lambs at a time.

Sometimes if a single had just arrived one of the triplets would be whipped over and rubbed thoroughly against the still wet single. It was surprising how many times these simple tactics worked.

"You would think that she would realise she'd only had one," Geordie would chuckle when both the new lambs were tucking in and mother stood with a contented smile on her face. "You see what happens when you can't count. You make sure you can do your sums."

There was though a regular supply of orphans who were in a pen in the steading and had to be fed by bottle. A lovely job, the pressure of the lamb's jaws sucking on the teat, thrusting against it to encourage more milk and all the time the taggly tail flailing with sheer ecstasy.

When a ewe had a dead lamb or when one died shortly after birth the corpse was whipped away, skinned and the skin fitted carefully onto one of the orphans. Holes were cut in the fresh coat for the legs of the impostor and cloaked with the smell of the dead infant the substitute was slipped gently in beside the grieving mother. There was a lot of sniffing, a lot of uncertainty, awkward questions about where have you been and sometimes flat refusal to be fooled. But most times the ruse worked and mother and child were released into the field, the lamb looking a bit ragged but having an advantage over all the others – he had an extra warm coat.

Even the ewes who did not at first accept the stranger wished upon her usually gave their blessing to the adoption after a while in the pen together. Sometimes the lamb took a few butts but hunger made them courageous and perhaps pressure of milk helped the ewe to make up her mind.

The lambing was succeeded by a couple of processes, which I did not greatly enjoy but that did not stop me being there. Tails and testicles were removed. When first I was present at these proceedings it was a bloody job with knives. Later it involved more pleasing rubber bands – strategically placed these starved the scrotum and the tail of blood and they simply withered away. Whether it was less painful for the animal I do not know but it was certainly less painful for the spectator.

The clipping was a major operation.

There was huge skill involved in clipping the fleece off a big, active sheep. Nowadays there are electric clippers that skim the skin and smoothly remove the fleece. The hand clippers were much more testing. Sprung so that they always wanted to be open it took great hand strength to use them all day. And they were gruesomely sharp.

There were two jobs at the clipping, which were fitted to the very old, and the very young.

One was tar. Tar was the cure all for sheep. When they had foot rot and the hoof needed trimming, the job was completed by the application of a dollop of tar. At the clipping, when a sheep got a snip, as happened to even the best clipper, the cry went up "Tar!" and the bod in charge of the tar raced over and dabbed all-healing tar on the wound.. The skill of the clipper was measured by how often he shouted "Tar!".

The other good job was the buist. Like the tar job it was guaranteed to get the operator dirty. All the better for that!

When the fleece was removed the cry was "Buist!". The operation was similar to branding but without the heat and scorch. Our brand was a circle with a capital "I" in the middle. Dipped in red paint, which gloried for some reason in the name of 'buist', it lay in a tray and when needed was stamped on the newly white flank.

Two giant items, which were stored dusty and cobwebbed in the steading, got their annual day out for the clipping.

One was a big, heavy table, which took four men to carry it out. The fanks where the clipping took place was at the far side of the stack yard from the square and it was every year a source of some colourful language when it was carried out.

The table was for laying out, folding and rolling the fleeces. This was yet another area of expertise where Watt excelled – was there no end to the man's talents? The trick of the fleece rolling was gently pulling out and turning a rope of wool from the edge of the fleece so that when it was tightly rolled the rope went round and tucked into itself to keep the roll tight. It was skilful work but Watt made it look easy.

The other dusty piece of equipment rolled out was even more cumbersome and a major piece of engineering to erect. It was a tall wig-wam skeleton of metal with, at the top, four big hooks. It was onto these that the woolsacks were fixed.

When full the sacks were the size of a saloon car. The fleeces were tossed in and when it looked like it would take no more one of the boys – sometimes me – was hoisted up and jumped into the greasy soft cushion of wool and had to jump up and down to pack it really tightly. Then a few more fleeces were tossed up and tramped down. When finally the bag was full to the brim it was let gently down, the boy allowed to escape and with a massive needle and a length of twine it was sewn closed and an empty sack was erected.

The sacks were dragged into the steading and a few days after the clipping was done a lorry came to collect them and take them off to Hunter's Mill in Brora.

That was the first sheep harvest.

There was another session of chaos when the sheep were dipped. This one required the presence of the local bobby and Ken the Bobby would arrive majestically on his huge iron bicycle. When he ceremoniously removed his cycle clips the dipping could begin.

For the man doing the actual dipping it was a wet and smelly job. The sheep had to be totally immersed – Ken was there to make sure of that – and the man standing by the dip tank side, clothed in oil skins like an Arctic fisherman, had a long handled tool with a wide splayed base with which to dook each animal. A lot of the sheep slipped into the dip quietly and came out gently, spluttering but waiting until they were up the run to the holding fank before giving a good shake. Others dived and made a mighty splash and came out and immediately sprayed the area with a great shaking shower. These soaked the oilskin man and anyone else foolish enough to get too close. There was quiet delight all round when Ken got a douche. "That's you louse free then, Ken," someone shouted and everyone except Ken laughed.

When the last sheep was done the dogs were dipped. It seemed to me to be an act of treachery after all they had done to help.

"It'll keep them clear of ticks and fleas for weeks," Geordie said.

The dogs shook themselves and looked at us reproachfully but their offended mood passed quickly and they frolicked around to dry and the betrayal was forgotten and not mentioned again.

On the deep, damp soil of Invercarron foot rot was a constant threat to the sheep. They were regularly brought in through the fank and had their hooves trimmed. It involved them in an undignified operation of being upended and having their hooves trimmed with a knife. If foot rot was visible – or smellable –then a dollop of purple ointment was rubbed in, followed by a splodge of tar. It did the trick.

The separation of the lambs from the ewes was a noisy business. Late into the evening the chorus of baas from different fields went on and on. "Poor things", Mother said. But by morning the cries had ceased and the lambs had magically become gimmers and hogs.

Most of them were sent off to the lamb sale in Lairg – the biggest one-day sale in Europe we were told repeatedly – a miracle of organisation and logistics.

It was the big sheep harvest. Prices were scrutinised in the paper. Compared with farms round about – Culrain, Gledfield, Poplars and Creich and bank balances all took a healthy surge.

Most of the lambs went south. All through the night of the sale there was a traffic of goods trains heading past us. It was the only night of the year on which, if sleepless, we could, instead of counting sheep, count sheep trains.

All year, in the wee field beside our green, a dozen tups had relaxed. Fed the best, they chewed the cud listlessly and in the summer sunned themselves like big, fat walruses. They were noble beasts. Heads held high they had noses like Roman Emperors – "Man, look at the head on him!" Old Duncan would say with delight. He like Roman noses on sheep. One, which displayed what he described as, a "pig snout" was off the place at the first opportunity.

Now the tups were called into action. Snorting and flaring their nostrils they trotted through their harems checking the stock like housewives feeling the loaves.

Not all the lambs had gone to Lairg. Some gimmers were kept and would later join and rejuvenate the stock of ewes. The hogs would be filled with turnips and corn over the winter and end up at the

Dingwall Mart where the buyers were not dealers but butchers.

On a weekend Mother would have a big pan of broth on the range and dig out of it a steaming chunk of mutton. The broth was rich with meat flavour and the meat, greyish coloured and having given up much of its taste to the broth, was sliced up and shared accompanied by tatties and cabbage and sometimes carrots. We were an H.P. sauce family – I had checked with Hamish and apparently his was a tomato sauce zone – and it was doused over all to give a bit of flavour.

"Steady," Mother would chide when we were too vigorous with the bottle.

That, I suppose, was the final sheep harvest and outside the snowdrops and primroses were just coming into flower – could the lambs be far behind?

FISHING

Considering that we lived a stone's throw from one of the best salmon rivers in Scotland we boys were remarkably coy about trying to catch a salmon..

Sure we would lean over the parapet of the bridge and see the dark shapes swaying in the water below and say things like, 'If I had a net...' or 'a gaff would reach that big fellow at the edge', but it never went further than that.

Hamish and I spent a lot of time hanging over the bridge parapet. One day, on our way home from school, we leaned over and saw that Admiral MacNamara was down below fishing and as we watched he hooked a salmon. We watched for a while as he played the fish, which shot back and fore across the pool, and we could see it clearly from above. MacNamara looked up and saw his audience and waved us down. "A hand..." we thought he said.

"He'll be wanting one of us to use the landing net," Hamish said.

"Should we go down?"

"Naw," Hamish pushed off his bike. "He's got that bloody doug with him."

It was not known what the Admiral thought of that episode.

Our fishing was more modest. The equipment very basic. In the Chemists in Bonar they sold ready connected hooks on a few inches of gut. Those we purchased and attached to a few yards of line and then rolled it onto a piece of stick. With the hook pushed into the stick end the whole lot fitted into a trouser pocket without difficulty. In the other pocket there was a tobacco tin with a few freshly dug worms and that completed the preparation.

The main venue was the Kyle. It was tidal and the shore was littered with bays, most of them muddy and shallow. The best time was supposedly when the tide was coming in but if we wandered down and it was past high water –Hey! – We just carried on anyway.

The method was not energetic. Find a suitable stone – that was not a round one, the line tended to slip off a round one – and tie the line around it a couple of feet shy of the hook. Unroll the line and put a big stone on top of the stick on the bank. The line was, of course, attached to the stick and a big stone was necessary in case we hooked Mobey Dick. Then run the poor worm onto the hook and throw hook and stone as far out as we could manage. Then it was a waiting game. If it was just Hamish, and myself and it usually was, we would tramp along to the next bay and launch another line into it. Then, unhurriedly, back to the first one and pull it in. Nine times out of ten we would have nothing. Sometimes the worm had been nibbled, which cheered us no end, but no catch materialised. But there were fish to be caught. The most common by a mile were flounders. They loved the muddy bays and were not the brightest of fish. Sometimes it was an eel. Oh! How we hated eels. They were demons. They screwed themselves into knots and destroyed our gut and lines. Their teeth were vicious and dangerous so getting the hook out was fraught with danger. When eventually we got the slimy devil off we were brutal in our response – the eel was chopped up with our pocketknives on a stone and thrown on the bank for the seagulls to gorge on.

In the long summer evenings with the sun thinking of sinking behind Carbisdale Castle – but hesitating – we wandered back and fore through the whins from one line to the other. Ceaselessly chatting about God knows what!

The great thing about flounders was they came closer to being a convenience food than any other fish. They packed their gut right beside their head – one strategic cut and it was ready for the frying pan. And when fried it was a simple task to skim the flaky, white meat away from the single big bone – no needle splinters, no picking of nasty spurs from teeth. The only drawback to this otherwise perfect fish was that it tasted of the mud in which it lived.

There must have been something in the air in the summer, which drove Hamish and I to invest huge amounts of time and effort to totally unproductive fishing.

We collected worms – round the damper corners of the square, where there was maybe a faulty guttering and a few rotting sacks lying in a shady corner – was best. Then mounting our bikes with our line, gut and hook on a stick in our pockets, off we went to burns all over the place.

The burn at Culrain practically dried up in late summer and there was a pool close under the railway bridge, with a dead tree in the bank. Below that tree, when the burn was empty save for the deeper places, the last wee trout hid. If we lay on the tree trunk and reached underneath we could catch and pull out the trapped tiddlers – for sadly tiddlers they were. Most times we just looked at their gasping despair and put them back. Not, I should add, from any sense of conservation or pity, but simply that if we took them home our mothers would refuse to cook them. There was too the knowledge that what they lacked in size was more than compensated for by the number of bones.

While there was still water in the burn there were several nice pools. We would drop our wormed hooks in at the top of the pool and let it slowly, very slowly, drift down with the current. There were usually a few minnows scudding around in the clear water. Had there been a decent trout in the pool it would have been visible at a glance so goodness knows where we expected our catch to appear.

But lying there on the short grass, with the sun beating down and the heat rising from the earth I suppose we thought anything was possible.

On such a day of shimmering heat we lay by the pool watching a dragonfly – fishing forgotten.

The dragonfly was showing off. He was big and he dived and turned and hovered, shimmering silver and blue, over the water.

"He's a big one."

"Aye."

He dipped to touch the surface of the water and rose straight up like a helicopter taking off. His wings were a silver haze but his big long body was blue and sparkling.

"He's bonny."

"Aye".

For a while he entertained us and we lay still and then as suddenly as he had arrived he was gone, flickering up the burn.

"Look."

In the pool we were suddenly aware that there lurked a monster. He had not been there before but perhaps he too had come out to look at the dragonfly.

"He's a whopper."

"Aye."

From the stones in the far side of the pool, only a couple of yards from us had appeared an eel's head. The beady black eyes were fixed on us and the expression was one of disdain.

"Cheeky bugger!"

"Aye."

We tossed a line into the water and waited for the giant to be tempted. Why we would want to catch an eel I cannot say. We would avoid an eel at all costs at other times. This big, fierce, slimy terror would for sure destroy out gear. This fellow watched us and our passing worm with motionless disdain.

"Wait." Hamish was up and off up the bank, and back down the other side so that he was on the bank directly above the eel.

Gently he unrolled a couple of yards of his line and dropped it softly into the water. The worm drifted gently past the eel's jaws but the head did not move nor the eyes flicker.

Hamish repeated the temptation several times but each time the result was the same.

"Bugger!" he shouted and pulled up his line.

He stormed off up the bank and returned humping the biggest stone he could carry. I knew what was coming and kept my eyes steadily on the target. Hamish aimed and adjusted and aimed again.

The pool shattered and flew in sparkling shards into the air. The bottom of the pool was lost in swirls of disturbed peat and it took a wee while for it to settle. When it did the eel remained unmoved, a surly look on his face.

"He's still there."

"Aye," Hamish snarled and headed off for another stone.

This time when the water cleared the eel was gone.

"Got him!" Hamish said but we both knew that he hadn't.

"Aye," I agreed.

There was no end of burns to test. We would mount our bikes and set off. Always the weather was hot and dry – if it was raining we just did not go but went down to the square and mooched about there. We were fair weather fishers.

The bigger jaunts were always in the summer holidays. The school bag was emptied out and Mother gave me a piece wrapped in greaseproof paper. Hamish would be similarly prepared and we would be given pennies to get a bottle of pop. Fortunately both Hamish and I favoured "Cream Soda" so that choice was never an issue. Who put the heavy bottle into their bag sometimes was. Hamish was a few months older than me and in such a situation he sometimes used his seniority.

We dabbed our hooks in the burn beside Cooper's at Mid Fearn and went up the Struie and tried our luck in the burn that comes out at Brooke's. Nothing stuck in the memory from these jaunts.

What we called Pirie's Burn (because a fellow, older, pupil of that name lived beside it) was actually officially Kincardine Burn. It was along by the East Church. The bridge, which took the main road over it, was the 'Fairy Bridge' – the stones on the top of the parapet had carved in little footprints, a bit big for fairies I thought. Whoever made them was heavy footed.

We dumped our bikes by the bridge and went upstream. We had been there many times. The furthest we went upstream led to a single high waterfall, which fell into a big, dark pool. Neither of us liked that spot. Even on the sunniest warmest day it was cool and dark and damp with water dripping from the fern strewn rock face. It was in a word 'spooky' so that was our only visit that far up.

Just yards up from the bridge there was a much more pleasant pool. A waterfall too fed it but it was a low and wide one. The trees stood respectfully back so that it was bright and cheery.

We came there one day and were surprised to find the burn nearly in spate. The water was brown in the fall and the pool had two big coverings of foam where the current swung round.

"I'll take the far side," Hamish announced. Age advantage usually gave him first choice.

I had baited my hook as he clambered across the rocks below the pool. As I was unrolling the line from the stick the hook fell through the surface of foam into the water, right at the edge. I had a few feet of line unrolled; enough to throw the hook out into midstream and pulled up the hook in preparation to throw it out.

As the worm appeared above the foam it was followed by a gaping mouth and big head. I was astonished. I simply dropped the hook back in and immediately it shot the line across the pool. I hung on and watched the line cutting circles and curves all over the pool. I must have yelled for Hamish stopped his rock trek to watch open-mouthed.

I concentrated on keeping the line as tight as I could and gradually the circling got slower.

"Get down to the shingle," Hamish was yelling and returning to my side of the burn.

Gradually I sidled down the bank and jumped onto the bank of shingle at the foot of the pool.

I could feel the resistance lessening and was gently bringing my catch towards me.

Hamish had arrived at my side.

"Slide him onto the stones!" He had to shout to make himself heard above the waterfall but his volume was too high even for that.

I backed away from the water's edge and pulled the line slowly in. The trout gave a final panic thrashing as it left the water but I pulled and Hamish pounced and our catch was secure.

We both bent over the prize. We were stunned into silence and just stared at the gleaming beauty of it. And the size! It was over a foot long. This was a fish away out of our league.

Carefully we wrapped it in leaves and put it in my school bag.

For a while we sat on the bank unwilling to close the occasion. We swigged Cream Soda and ate our pieces.

"What a beauty!"

"Aye."

"That's the biggest ever."

"By a mile".

"Aye."

"Will there be more?'

"I doubt it."

"We better give it a try."

"Aye."

Without great expectation of another miracle we cast our hooks out and let the current bring them round.

The afternoon wove on and no other giant trout – or pigmy one – came near us.

We packed up and headed back down to the bridge. A nice car was on the verge beside the road. A big man in a tweed jacket was watching our approach.

"Any luck boys?" he called as we clambered up beside the bridge.

"Aye," Hamish said casually. "We got one."

"One?" The man was smirking. "I didn't think there would be much in there."

"Do you want to see it?" Hamish invited innocently.

"Big one?" The man was laughing now.

"Show him, Willie," Hamish nodded to me.

I undid my bag and emptied the contents out onto the grass and pulled the leaves back to reveal my prize.

"Good God!" The man knelt beside me and stroked the long body. "That is a nice one. I never thought of trying this wee burn. What fly? And, hey," he looked around, "Where's your rods?"

"No rods," Hamish produced his rolled up line from his pocket.

"A worm," I said.

"Good God!" repeated the man. "Is this the first you've got in here?"

"Ach, no," Hamish laughed; he had appointed himself PR officer. "We get a few in here."

"Not as big as this?"

"Oh, aye," Hamish laughed out loud. "There's a few big fellows in there."

We never did get another in Pirie's Burn – bigger or smaller.

"The big fellow wi' the car must have fished it out," Hamish said.

MUSIC

There must be something in the Highland heart, which is stirred by bagpipe music. I know that it is not to everyone's taste but then very few things do suit all tastes.

My first memories of pipes were when we made our trip to the Highland Games in Dornoch. We caught the bus in Ardgay and went upstairs – for it was to be a day of treats – and squirmed with excitement on the wooden utility seats.

As we neared Dornoch the bus filled and the excitement grew.

"What a lovely day."

"Aye, aren't they lucky."

"Where's your kilt, young man?"

And then we were coming into Dornoch. Over to our right we could see the tents in the games field and, the windows being open, we could hear the pipes.

There were the pibroach pipes- haunting and slow and, though aimed at the piping elite, still stirring and evocative of Scotland's ancient tragedies to even the average listener.

Then there was the accompaniment to the dancers. Jigs and reels, which challenged even the most unmusical foot not to tap. And then there were the solo competitions – serious men who fiddled with drones and tuned and twiddled and finally broke into a stately promenade around the wooden platform and tried their best to impress a couple of ancients in old army forage caps who had played and listened to pipes for sixty, maybe seventy, years. They knew every grace note and every burl, and could tell a winner with their eyes closed.

Several times during the day, the Pipe Band would take to the field. Sadly in Dornoch there was usually just the local band. Go to Invergordon or Strathpeffer Games, they told me, because there they had enough bands to have a real competition. The story goes that Dornoch's competition foundered when Dornoch Band won for the umpteenth time.

Which, on the evidence, I witnessed was not a surprise. They certainly lifted my heart to such an extent that an ambition to be a piper was founded.

It did not happen straight away. My parents, rightly I now allow, waited to see if this was just a passing fancy. But I was stubborn and persistent.

A precursor to learning the pipes is learning to play the chanter. To differentiate it from the note playing part of the pipes, which is also called the chanter, the starting tool is a practice chanter. Made of wood, it is in two parts, which slot together. The mouthpiece is an expanded tube which fits over the reed at the top of the main part of the instrument. There are eight finger holes down the front and a single hole on the back so only the thumb of the right hand is not actively playing a part.

Musical instruments were not on the school curriculum.

My sister Barbara had taken up the violin and Miss Brown in Ardgay taught her. We all shared Barbara's agony as she scraped out the scales and finally got a tune – there was a huge relief.

When Barbara's tortures were over it was my turn to take up the turning of the screw.

I was sent to a man named MacKay who was the manager of the Caley Hotel in Bonar but, strangely, could manage too to take a wee class of chanter pupils on a Saturday night.

The logistics of my Saturday night class were complicated. I cycled from home to the junction of our Strathkyle road with the Strathcarron one. There I was picked up by Johnie D's father, Johnie being a fellow pupil, and after the class was over I was dropped off again, retrieved my bike from behind the snow-plough and pedaled like a fury home.

Pedalling through the dark was terror. All the way I was going through woods and sounds and scuffles pursued me mercilessly. One night my cheek was brushed gently and before I realised that it was the caress of an owl's wing I may well have screamed.

Bad though that was it was nowhere near as bad as standing in the dark waiting for my lift. I heartily regretted the foolishness, which had led me to take part in this weekly punishment.

The scales were painfully mastered and I was set to learn my first tune. It was "Lord Lovat's Lament" which, in spite of its dreary title was actually a march. It was the first tune in the book and Mr MacKay was a believer in doing things by the book.

"Drr-um" he sighed. "Give it some body. A birl has to birl or it's no a birl."

Then Mr MacKay ceased his lessons. If it was because my birls did not birl I cannot say. I hope that it was because he realised that as manager of the Caley he might use his Saturday evenings to more rewarding ends.

We the pupils were passed on to Andy Murray and learned a few more tunes and were pushed onto the next rung of the ladder – coming to terms with the real thing – bagpipes.

122

The purchase of a set of bagpipes was a major undertaking and must have cost my parents and perhaps my siblings a tightening of their belts, which at the time I did not appreciate at all.

The pipes were ordered from Hugh MacPherson in Edinburgh – by all accounts a man who hailed originally from Sutherland and was therefore trustworthy. They arrived in a stout wooden case, which was reminiscent of a small coffin.

That marked the beginning of a period of great suffering for my family and the neighbours. A learner on the pipes is a demon arrived straight from hell.

I will not linger on the suffering I inflicted. I did eventually improve and could manage a passable tune.

When Invercarron House gardener John Thain departed a man called Bratchie replaced him. I do not think he had a first name. He was from the south of Scotland and spoke a language of his own but, sadly for me, he heard my piping efforts, spoke to my father about it and I was sent off down every week to give him a few tunes.

His wife was a tiny grey woman who sat by the fire and smiled bravely while I played in their little sitting room. Then she would rise and go through to the kitchen and a long time after would reappear with a tray and I would pack away my pipes while she laid out the cups and saucers and teapot. Then we would sit in awkward silence together and drink tea and have a biscuit each.

One evening when I arrived there was already a pipe case on the table.

"Let's show ye this," Bratchie unclipped the case.

My pipes were run of the mill stainless steel mounted with fake ivory trims at the top of the drones and at the base of the chanter. I had seen a set bedecked in silver – everywhere that I had steel and ivory was silver figures with thistles – very nice but nothing I craved. These were apparently called "half mounted pipes". There was obviously "full mounted' sets about but I had never seen one.

This set, which Bratchie unveiled proudly, was "full mounted" but not in silver – these were gold. They both looked at me expectantly, so I did my best at enthusiastic awe – and it was quite good, I thought.

"Braw, eh?" Bratchie was putting the drones on.

Every available space on the pipes was covered in gold, engraved with flags and thistles and it was ugly. If I knew the word 'ostentatious' I would have thought it – in fact when I did later learn the word I immediately thought of Bratchie's pipes.

"They've not been played for forty years," Mrs Bratchie said as if that was the icing on the cake. "Beautiful aren't they," she spoke as if referring to children.

"You'll no see mony sets like this," Bratchie laid them out reverently on the table. He was the kind of man who, if he had a car, would have a personalised number.

The pipes were duly admired for a few more minutes then they were carefully taken apart, wrapped in clean, fluffy dusters and laid to rest in the case. Bratchie carried the wee coffin out and up the stairs and buried them for another forty years.

I have never come across anyone who has seen a gold mounted set. Most, even seasoned pipers, think that I have got it wrong. "Silver mounted" they correct me gently. I know, however, that out there somewhere there is at least one ugly fully gold mounted set.

In the summer, when Bratchie was busy in the garden, I would join him there.

The paths in the garden were manicured lawn and in the evening I would march up and down while Bratchie worked amongst the flowers and vegetables.

What the poor birds thought of this horrendous intrusion into the stillness of the evening cannot be imagined.

Bratchie was an uncritical listener. His reaction was usually no more than a nod. His total usefulness to me was to encourage me to practice.

I would like to say that I later won several gold medals at the Northern Meetings for pibroach and march. And similar awards at Dornoch, Strathpeffer, Invergordon and Braemar games.

But sadly it would be a lie. I was pretty useless.

I was the one who gave the lie to the saying that practice makes perfect. No matter how much I was pressed into practice I was not a huge success. I did eventually join the Bonar Ardgay Pipe Band but was never good enough to be a soloist.

One of my greatest skills was 'goosing'. It is possible to keep the pipe drones working and by turning the chanter in towards one's body to cut it off. With skill like that I could very convincingly still work my fingers on the chanter and give the impression that I was playing along. My big drawback was that all the tunes in the band's repertoire had to be memorised and I simply could not do it. A march or a slow march I did not mind too much but jigs and strathspeys and those fast things were a bridge too far.

A young couple with two very little children arrived and moved in next door to Bratchie's. He had been in the Royal Navy and had come as a driver/valet/dogsbody for Admiral MacNamara. His name was Sidney Sweet and his wife was Samantha – shortened to Sam. Thankfully with a name like Sweet the children were both girls.

I made myself known to them and got into the habit of

wandering down to visit them some evenings. Sid was happy in his job but poor Sam was miserable. Imagine the poor lassie dropped into the middle of nowhere with the Bratchies for neighbours – he gruff and talking in an unknown tongue and she a hermit who ventured out no further than the clothes line but fled back into the house if anyone should appear while she was out there.

I would have liked Sam better if she was not so hopelessly English – she could not be told that the Royal Navy was not the English Navy but the British Navy.

"My brother Peter is in the Navy and he certainly isn't English', I told her one evening when Sid had popped off up to the Big House to 'tuck the Admiral in' as he said.

"Oh, I know," Sam agreed. "There are lots of British men in the Navy. There's some Irish too – like the Admiral."

I sighed and tried again. Maybe she would be less possessive of the Army.

"And what about 'The Seaforths', 'The Black Watch' and all those Scottish regiments? – They're not English."

"No, of course not. They're like the Americans and the Australians. They're not English but they fought for England in the war."

"You'll never get through," Sid was back and laughing at our repeated debate. "Let's put the kettle on and then we'll have a couple of records."

That was really why I was there. In pride of place in their room was a beautiful wood radiogram. It stood solidly on the floor with a record cupboard built in and the top lifted up to reveal a state of the art turn table at one side and radio controls at the other.

I was not always enthusiastic about the music available. I did not understand or like jazz then and do not like or understand it now. Sid's other enthusiasm was for military and brass bands and I liked them too. "Can't you just see the Marine Band?" he would say but I couldn't.

"Lovely," Sam would say and smile at Sid who would give her a hug and wink at me. I realised that he knew that she was thick but loved her just the same.

It was hardly a surprise when Sid told me that they were leaving. Sam was humming as she packed a box, which she had recently unpacked.

"Where are you going?"

"Home," said Sam happily.

"Portsmouth," said Sid. "The Admiral has been very good – he's got me a chance of a job down there with one of his cronies."

"That's good."

"Nice of him," Sam said.

"He knew how things were here," Sid raised an eyebrow and I knew what he meant.

"Away from them weirdos next door," Sam said. "Do you know no one ever visits them?"

"I do, " I said.

"You're the only one that visits us too," Sid laughed.

"When are you off?" I felt from the enthusiasm of Sam's packing that it could be next day.

"End of the month – a couple of weeks yet," Sam said and the length of the remaining sentence seemed to depress her.

"Do you want to buy the radiogram?" Sid asked me.

"Oh, I dunno," I was surprised – it seemed to be their prize possession.

"We can't take it – it's too big."

"But your furniture…?"

"It's not ours – the radiogram is the only thing that is ours."

"I would need to ask."

"Sure – tell them thirty quid and I'll throw in a few records."

I did ask. Father said to offer twenty but he was overruled by Mother – "Poor things – they'll need every penny they can get – offer twenty five."

I did and Sid readily accepted and we wheeled the radiogram up to our house on a flat trolley.

Mother had not seen it before so I was anxious for approval.

"Oh, it's lovely!" Mother gushed as we carried it in and put it under the window. "Wait!" She rushed off to the bedroom and came back with a fiver – I had already handed over the agreed twenty-five – and she handed it to Sid. "I didn't realise it was so big – and so smart. I couldn't enjoy it if I thought we'd done you."

So we became owners of a very grand radiogram which Mother and I knew had cost thirty quid but Father was pleased to believe that he had got for a bargain price of twenty-five.

When Usdean and Marie moved out and went to Bonar their farm cottage was rented to a couple of pensioners – the Gordons. Robert Gordon – called Bob by the farm men – was a quiet little man. He was a pipe smoker but his wife; a witch woman, objected and Gordon had to smoke his pipe at the gable end. In deepest winter, with snow hurtling in the wind, if we were out at night, we might see the tiny glow of his pipe at the house end – "Poor man," Mother would say.

I do not know quite how it came about but I became a regular visitor. All the more strange for Mrs Gordon hated all children and shouted at Hamish and his siblings when ever she saw them. I do not recall being a particularly precocious child but there was I the only visitor to the Bratchies and the Sweets and now to the Gordons.

Mrs Gordon was strange. I did not need Hamish to tell me. I knew enough to know that she would speak to me of things that frankly I would rather not know about. Like the friend of hers who had such a job weaning her child off the breast that she frightened the child away by draping a rabbit shin strategically. It was not something that I wanted to know.

Another of her monologues to me concerned the effect of the moon on the likelihood of women becoming pregnant. If I remember right it was her contention that women would not get pregnant while the moon was waxing – or could it have been waning, now I cannot remember so don't take my word for it.

"If people knew that and acted on it there wouldn't be broods like next door."

Hamish's family lived next door and he was one of the brood of six referred to. The Gordons had no children so if that was their wish then maybe it was the result of abstaining from sex for half the month. Maybe, of course, knowing her, it was because they abstained for the whole month.

It was not a subject that I was comfortable with though even then I could see the flaw – birthdays were all through the month. I thought it wiser to just let it pass.

I'm not sure why I kept visiting. In truth I did not like her. My mother disapproved of her and did not know I visited as much as I did.

When I told the Gordons that we had acquired a radiogram she was immediately interested.

"We used to have a gramophone but the spring broke," she lamented.

"That's a pity," I comforted.

"We have piles of records – oh, some really funny ones," Mrs Gordon laughed just thinking of them. "You can have them."

There were indeed a lot of records – piles of 78s, which weighed a ton. It took me several trips to take them over the field home.

"I'm no sure about this," my mother said each time I struggled in with another batch.

"It's OK," I lied, "they were going to dump them."

There were lots of records of Scottish Dance music – Ian Powrie, Jim MacLeod, Jimmy Shand and the like, which we all liked.

And then there was a pile of what Mrs G. had been referring to as the funny ones. I am not sure if one would say they were of comedians singing or singers trying to be comedians. Will Fyffe, Harry Lauder were already know to us but there was a stranger called Don

Dallas who sang drunken songs and was either very drunk when he sang them or very good at acting drunk.

In the middle of a song these men would break off and tell a few jokes and then get on with the song.

One of Dallas's jokes was how while out first footing at New Year with his whisky bottle in his pocket he had slipped on the ice and fallen. As he arose he felt something trickling down his leg – "Oh! Lord! Let it be blood."

One of his songs rendered in a rasping slur went:

"Twelve and a tanner a bottle,

That's what it's costing the day.

Twelve and a tanner a bottle,

It tak's all the pleasure away.

Before you can get a wee drappie,

You have to spend all that you've got.

How can a fellow be happy?

When happiness cost such a lot?"

There was too a record of "Grannie's Heilan' Hame". We forgave McFarlane for his strange accent and were a wee bit flattered that he should mention Embo, Dornoch, Skelbo, Golspie and Tain. It was our first taste of celebrity.

Mrs Gordon asked regularly which records we had listened to. "When I replied, "Don Dallas," she howled with laughter.

"Isn't he s scream?"

"He sounds drunk," I said.

"No, no – he's just acting. Such a clever man."

I had my doubts but kept them to myself.

"I best be off – I've got homework."

I went out into the darkness. A strong west wind was lashing across the front of the house and I set off at a run for home.

"Goodnight, Boy," Old Gordon's voice came from the gable end where he carefully sheltered his pipe from the rain.

"Goodnight," I called against the wind.

WINTER

The final harvest of the year was the potatoes - an important enough harvest to justify its own school holiday –"the Tattie Holidays".

The heady heat of the summer had faded into the cool mists of autumn and the soil in the potato fields turned to mud.

Invercarron did not go in for spuds in a big way. What were grown were for the use of the families who had helped on a few days or evenings at corn harvest time, or with the hay and any other job where help could be given. The pay back was not just tatties but turnips and the use of a tractor and trailer for bringing sticks down from the hill.

It was still a communal effort to lift the tatties. Bags were delivered to each house, ours, Gordon's Hamish's and stored either in a shed, under a heap of blankets and coats, or, in the case of Gordon's, in the wee cubby hole under the stairs.

What was left was pitted – a long trench, about six feet wide and a couple of feet deep was dug and lined with straw. The spuds were piled in and built up into a long pyramid and this, too, was covered in straw before the whole thing was topped off with a good layer of soil – that should keep the contents safe from frost and, always, as far as I knew, did. As much to do, no doubt, to the humming and hawing and looking at the sky, which preceded, opening the pit in the winter.

My father, of course, grew potatoes in the garden. There, however, they were mainly earlies and maybe a row or two of Golden Wonders to please mother, who thought they were the best.

Unlike Invercarron, Mid Fearn had a whole field of potatoes and that took a big squad to lift. As well as we school kids there were women from Ardgay and Tain.

I landed on my feet there – "Who can drive a tractor?" the foreman shouted on the first morning and my hand was up while the others were still debating the possible drawbacks.

So I got the job of slowly driving a tractor – a Fergie – and trailer up and down the field while the men gathered the baskets of spuds from the pickers and emptied them into the trailer. It was a superb job, which was made even better by the envious looks from my school friends.

Brooke, who farmed Mid Fearn, was obviously a man with good contacts for our dinner was brought from the Tain school canteen in big steel containers. As far as I can recall it was mince and tatties everyday but I would be the last person to complain about that – mince and tatties were to me as good as dinners could get.

Another tractor job that fell to me at that time of year was when the dung was going out onto the fields.

Clearing the folds of fully six feet of dung was a major undertaking. It was done by grape and sheer hard labour at first but then they got a shovel for the front of the Fergie. The big back wheels had to be filled with water to balance the weight of lifting the forks full of dung but it saved a massive amount of backbreaking labour.

The dung was still taken out to the fields and unloaded into little heaps every few yards. That is where I came in – I could drive the tractor for a few yards, stop while the dung was dragged off the trailer and then move on a few yards and let another wee heap be deposited.

The hard work of spreading the heaps by grape remained but thankfully that was not considered boy's work. It was when the dung was evenly spread that the ploughing could begin.

By that time we were trapped by the dark. No time for a wander to the square after school and only a few hours available at the weekends.

As soon as it was light the stock had to be fed. Not that light was very evident. It was a steel coloured day with a lowering sky and a freezing wind - a wind that penetrated to the bones and gnawed at the marrow. Too cold for snow but flurries of hail shrapnelled in on the wind and lay in little drifts on the frozen earth and stirred and twirled like venomous sand.

The sheep needed no calling to come for their food. They were spread across the ridged field gnawing on frozen turnips, which were ice welded into the soil, but when they heard the sound of the Fergie they began to run. By the time I reached the feeding troughs all but the lamest ones was milling around the tractor and trailer. I forked hay into the hakes, and then jumped down and shouldered the bag of oats and nuts.

As I walked along the line of feed boxes I poured an even ration along each trough. Not as easy as it sounds with anxious animals trying to push me aside and trip me up. No Christmas spirit from these - and I would not expect it from these evil possessors of the devil's eyes and smoking nostrils.

No shelter here. The wind, zipping the hail across the rutted field, hissed and spat. I pitied the sheep but they turned their scornful eyes and I knew that they preferred this iron, hoof-tapping ground to the previous weeks of deep, heavy mud and rain soaked fleeces.

I closed the door and stood in the gloom relishing the change. The wind rattled the door and the corrugated iron roof but there in the byre it was warm with body heat and gusting breath and sweet with the smell of hay and fresh dung.

I clicked the light switch and two dim bulbs glowed dustily - creating more shadow than light. Big horned heads turned in my direction and paused their chewing jaws for one beat - no more.

Down the row of stalls I went, scraping the soiled straw and dung into the gutter. Shouldering aside the more obstinate rears, wary round the hind end of the red, rogue kicker, the grape ringing on the concrete. Then brush and grape to clear the gutter and back and fore to the barn with fresh straw to renew the bedding - an extra armful to the calves to allow for cosy nests. Hay, full of clover and some sharp thistles, smelling of a dusty summer, I piled into the hakes above the cows heads.

Turnips, split in the finger-threatening cutter, emptied by the basketful in the feeding troughs in front of each beast caused a rising chorus of crunching. I checked the water and then stood back.

The calves, standing watchful on big-kneed legs, suddenly pranced and danced or plunged beneath their mothers to assuage an amazingly sudden hunger.

One little fellow, dark rusty red faced me and with splayed legs looked ready for imminent flight. But when I stepped up to him he stood his dubious ground and allowed me to brush my hand over his curly head. It was his first Christmas. It was his only Christmas. As I paused he raised his pink mouth and enclosed it around my fingers, hard gums working. Soft brown eyes rolled in concentration and fluttering his long lashes - lashes a diva would die for.

Before next Christmas came these calves would have had their one brief summer in the fields and then be brought in to be coddled on boiled barley, bruised oats and treacle and curry brushed and polished before going to the fat stock shows. There they would be awarded rosettes and certificates, which would hang proudly beside them in the butchers' windows.

It didn't seem the right time to think about that. They were due nothing more but I went through to the bruiser and came back with bruised oats. It was a wee treat, which the cows licked up with relish and even as they sneezed on the dryness of it their tongues reached out for more.

But weekdays were school and home.

"I'll be glad to see the spring," Mother would moan. "I can't be doing with boys under my feet all the time."

That was not fair – what about the girls?

When we were still all at home the evenings were crowded. My mother and my sisters were clicking knitting needles for most of the time. We boys were occasionally enrolled to hold the hanks of wool while they rolled it into balls – "hurry up, my arms are breaking", "Hush and stop moaning."

"Lovely colour."

"Does it go?"

"Look at this," a magazine would be held up with a picture of a baby in a knitted hat. "Isn't that cute?"

"Who for?"

It was sometimes the problem – find something that they wanted to knit and then decide who it could be for. Peter and I would often become aware of being the subject of calculating appraisal – we were often conscious of being disappointments.

My main occupation was trying to keep up with Peter. If he was making crawling tractors from cotton reels, rubber bands and candles I wanted to assist.

"See if it'll climb that."

"Brrr…rrrrm."

"Too steep."

"Give it time….brrrm."

We sometimes had aircraft kits to build – balsa wood and paper. Huge concentration and long hours of work and the end result always disappointed. They never looked like the real thing.

Peter taught me to play draughts and we would have a go at snakes and ladders, ludo, cards and anything else that came our way. Occasionally we would get the girls to join in and then it was win at all cost.

Father meanwhile was patiently dismantling or putting back together a clock. Silently and meticulously he would work, ignoring the chat around him and then finally the clock would be started. The pendulum was attached and swung into action and he would sit and watch and listen – and smile when the clock chimed and we would all smile with him then.

We had one huge source of entertainment – my parents had invested in a full twenty volume set of the "Children's Encyclopaedia". It was a bottomless store of ideas for us all and even when my siblings had left home I still night after night ploughed through those books.

They covered everything and I learned huge chunks of trivia which has stayed with me ever since. Plus ancient history – Romans, Egyptians and so on – we were given loads of modern history and the rise of the British Empire. The books left no room for doubt that the British Empire was a blessing to the whole world.

There were features on the solar system and space with marvellous colour plate illustrations. There were stories – everything from Aesop to the Bible to Han Anderson. Art featured reproductions of paintings and pages of photographs of sculptures – I naturally lingered over the naked women and noted that all the men sported fig leaves – I was eventually surprised to see in real life a statue of a male without a leaf – it was quite a shock.

There were rousing articles about explorers – especially the British ones – the courage of Arctic desperados and the stubborn persistence of Bible wielding commandoes forcing their way into the jungles.

Every animal, fish and bird in the whole world was in there – that was how I knew that the circus 'giant rat' was a coypu. Every human society and nation was explained and illustrated and there was no end to the strange places people would live in and the strange things they would do. Those pages of the encyclopaedia came to life when, while I was still in the infants, we had a school visit by a big group from Carbisdale which by then was a Youth Hostel. It must have been some international rally of young people and a crowd of them visited us bedecked in their national costumes. It was the first time that I, and most of the other children, had seen a black or Asian person. Some of the outfits were colourful and exciting but several we thought dull and disappointing. I recall the representative of Canada, a country to which I had many family ties, wore mundane working clothes with a big hat. The Australian was no better – my idea of an Australian was a wee black man with a long wooden spear. The American representative of the USA was worst of all – we all wanted a Big Chief in robes and feathers, what we got was not even a cowboy, but a chap who looked fresh from the croft in a blue overall.

Christmas was not the frantic holiday spending spree that it has now developed into. Work went on much as usual – shops were open and postmen went on their rounds. Schools were closed, as were the banks, but then, as now, teachers and bankers were not recognised as members of the workers of the world.

In school we did put up decorations. These were our own make – hours were spent cutting sticky coloured paper into strips and making them into chains. They were actually very pretty and effective and we were proud of them.

The big acknowledgement of Christmas was the party in the Ardgay Hall. It was an orgy of games, which were trotted out at Christmas and then forgotten until the next year. They were designed to include everyone. There was 'The Farmer's in his Den'. A large circle sang and shuffled sideways while one embarrassed boy stood in the centre and took on the persona of the Farmer. The Farmer first chose a wife – cause for giggles and blushes – and then the wife chose a child.

The group in the centre of the circle grew as the child selected a dog and then the whole thing plunged into the ridiculous when the dog chose a bone and then we all boisterously patted the dog. For children brought up to pat a dog, to pat a bone was a new twist, which we never did understand.

Having gone through all that we would repeat the whole process again and again with a new farmer until nearly everyone had arrived in the centre as something or other.

There were more boisterous games like 'pass the parcel' and 'musical chairs' – they were rife with cheating and tears were not unknown. The parcel usually contained a bag of sweets or a bar of chocolate and it was generally accepted that it was a lot of work for a sweetie.

The games were followed by tea. Tables of sandwiches and cakes were spread and gigantic teapots were brought from the kitchen that was set up in Fergie's steading behind the Hall. Behaviour was always good, not because we were all angels but because most of our Mothers were on the serving squad and a look was enough to curb any signs of trouble.

When the food was done and the tables cleared the lights were dimmed and in the spooky darkness we could hear the jingling of sleigh bells outside. As they got nearer nerves began to jangle and some of the smaller children would burst into tears or, worse still, simply scream.

Then the door was thrown open and in a rush of icy air and a blitz of snowflakes the long robed Santa shuffled in. Hugely hooded and hugely bearded surely such a fearsome visitor would, on any other occasion, have been ejected from a children's gathering. Here he was lauded and cheered and even the older ones who knew that it was Alistair Aird joined in the excitement.

Then it was time to dole out the presents. Each name of every child in the parish was called out and in various degrees of confidence, fear and swagger we took our turn to go and receive our Christmas wrapped present.

Books were a popular choice. Girls were easy, dolls and ribbons and bows, boys were sometimes lucky and got a penknife or unlucky and got a packet of hankies. One year I was spectacularly delighted with a mouth organ.

When it was over Santa shuffled off out of the Hall and the lights were turned up again and it was time to get coats, scarves and bonnets on and then out into the howling dark with the torch beam an exciting frenzy of snowflakes.

Christmas day was marked by the overnight visit of Santa Clause, this time to the house. I was taken out into the snowy green on a Christmas morning and my father showed me the tracks of a sleigh in the snow, the footprints of the reindeer and, of course, the big boot marks of Santa himself. It must have been a Sunday if he was not at work – or maybe it was very early – there is no doubt I would have been up early on Christmas morning.

The filled stockings bore no massive treasures but each item was so very special having been delivered by sleigh. There was always an orange in the toe – an orange was rare and a treat. I usually got a drawing book and a colouring book and crayons or a little water colour paint set with a brush – Mother must have told Santa that I liked drawing and colouring and was quite good at it.

Christmas dinner was special only in the particular that the standard hen was roasted rather than boiled. In addition it was stuffed with oatmeal and onions and, because she had seen a picture in one of the magazines, we had an addition of sausages. Pudding was the dumpling – toasted before the fire to give it a good skin – topped with cream, which Jean had brought home from Bonar as a treat.

For New Year my father did have a day off. The meal of Christmas was reprised and we were given glasses of home made non-alcoholic ginger wine – thick and sweet like cough medicine.

Neighbours called during the day with a whisky bottle and Mother refused but Father accepted a dram and one was poured from our bottle for the visitor. Even I as the smallest person present was shaken by the hand and wished "A Guid New Year!"

Most of our visitors were sober enough – ours was not a party house so visits were short. We all dreaded Angie – he would hurtle precariously down the hill on his bike and land in our big box hedge by the road. He was even less steady off the bike and every year tried to kiss Mother and the girls and they all shrank away in terror – Poor Angie was not a gift to the ladies, his bottom lip hung like an open drawer and he dribbled – not an appealing kisser.

The period after New Year was usually the coldest. Snow was plentiful and we were not short of hills for sledging. There were plenty shallow ponds of fresh water in the fields which froze solid; in our tackety boots we slid and slid. "Keep the kettle boiling!" was the cry. The aim was to have at least one body hurtling down a slide at any time. It was like sliding on glass – the leaves of grass and thistles and clover trapped in the hard hand of the ice and the tickets roaring on the slide.

Rarely did snow stop us from getting to school but some of the children from the more remote glens did miss sometimes. Snow was not in itself the problem – the wind and the drift were what stopped things. Posties more than most felt the harshness of those conditions.

My Father rarely swore but "Stupid Bugger" he said to mother one day and she was mortified for the 'stupid bugger' to whom he referred was the Rev Mr MacDougall. The minister had consulted the radio forecast and decided that on the following Sunday conditions would not have improved from the raging blizzard so he would cancel his services. He felt obliged to write to the more distant members of the congregation to warn them of this decision – unchristianly forgetting that to reach those distant remote addresses required the postie to deliver it. Had you taken a popularity poll in the Post Office that week poor Mr MacDougall would have been right down in the basement?

And when that frost came – the one which froze the sap in the trees and the blood in your ears – even the Carron froze over. With exaggerated care we would venture out onto the ice and hear it groan but then confidence grew and we would dance and jump on the river – like Jesus in the Bible but we made no claims to holiness for it.

Then the thaw would come. At our back door we would stand in awe and listen to the growl and grind of the river ice melting. That same ice in its power had once before carried away a Bonar bridge and when we heard it growling we feared for the bridge and when I went to bed I pulled the blankets over my ears to shut out the threat.

And there was still a wee regret that the snow was going, that the slides would melt and that the trees and the hills would lose their cloaks of innocent beauty.

NO WELL

It has been my great good fortune to have spent almost all my life under the umbrella of the National Health Service. I know that without the medical expertise and care of that marvellous service my own life would have been over certainly ten years ago – and arguably sixty years ago. To To a whole squadron of helpers I owe my life.

My first brush with the service was while still very young – but only as a spectator.

My father's postie route at that time was Invercarron and up to Brae at the end of Strathkyle. In those days the curse of posties and other van drivers were the gates. Before the blessed arrival of cattle grids every track into every croft had a gate. The formula was always the same, stop, get out and open the gate, get back in and drive through and stop, get out, close the gate, get back into the van and go to the house. On return the process was repeated at equal length.

This particular day was around New Year and the snow had lain and frozen for a long time. In the gateway, which my father was negotiating, the snow had packed to ice. He had opened the gate and was about to get back into the van when, as he turned, he realised that the van was sliding forward. He ran round the front towards the driver's door but slipped on the ice and fell – and the van ran over his leg.

The crew of the ambulance, when they knew they were about to pass our road end made a detour down. In the dark depth of icy night we crept out and into the back of the bright ambulance. In a cocoon of grey blankets and white sheets a thin grey face tried to smile at us.

Many years later when they were discussing the awards of long service and safe driving certificates the heads of the Post Office considered this incident. Could a man lose a safe driving award for running over his own leg? Common sense prevailed and the certificate was awarded, framed and hung on the wall.

On that night in deep winter they took Father to the hospital in Golspie.

When Mother went to visit she had to take me too – the others were in school. It was an adventure. A visit beyond Dornoch was a daring trip into the unknown. In our layers of winter woollies we sat on the wooden utility seats of a Highland Bus and watched the snow muffled foreign fields slip by.

When we went up the hill to the hospital a surprise awaited us.

"No children, sorry," the nurse said. "But he wants to see his Daddy," Mother's appeal. "Sorry – rules."

So I was left outside in the snow while mother went into the ward.

I found that if I climbed up on a seat which was by the front wall – for relaxation of patients in the heady heat of summer – and then up on the back of it I could see into the ward. At the other side my father lay and saw me and smiled and waved and I waved frantically back. My mother saw me too and glanced around nervously at the passing nurses who glided like starched skaters across the shining ice floor.

"They all said it was a shame," my mother said sadly on the bus home. "They all said you could have come in – it would have done no harm".

It was in another winter – in the holiday days between Christmas and New Year – that I decided to move onto centre stage.

I seem to recall that the first sign of trouble was when our bedroom wall began to melt. I shared the smallest room and the small bed therein with Peter and this was the first time that the walls showed any sign of instability. They peeled in an array of jelly like tongues and as each tongue slipped away from the wall it revealed a screaming face, all bone and teeth and angry eyes. There was a lot of screaming too but, much later, Peter told me that it was me 'making a din'. There were moments of pleasure too – sometime I awoke to find a sister, Jean or Barbara, or maybe both, looking grim and saint like as they wiped my sweating brow with a damp cloth. They murmured softly and seemed very grown up and capable.

I was carted off in an ambulance on the last day of the year. When I was out of the house, Peter told me at the same time as he accused me of yelling, our room was sealed with a burning candle inside 'to get rid of the germs'. Peter had shared my bed all week but he did not share my scarlet fever.

I was taken to the hospital in Invergordon and because it was for infectious deceases it had a no visitor rule.

I stayed a long time. Other kids came and went but still I stayed in the corner. Nurses spoiled me and the weeks turned into months. The hold-up was my nose. The decease had swollen the inner part at the top of my nose restricting my breathing and I was not to be released until that had cleared.

Had they kept to that plan I would be there still for my nose never did clear and I have spent all my life as a mouth breather – a stigma which is associated, I believe, with mental illness.

It was the middle of March when the doctors finally gave up on my nose and my mother appeared to claim me.

March or no March there was no sign of spring – instead we had a spell of heavy snow. Mother said that I appeared from the hospital like 'a little waif'. I was certainly white and she was charitable enough not to draw attention to the fact that my hair hung down on my shoulders. No one had thought of getting it cut in the ward. It was the first job thrust on Father when he got home that night.

She had hired Jack Campbell's taxi to fetch me. It was a vastly flattering expense. The car was a big Ford Pilot and we sat in the deep leather seats in the back as the chains on the wheels throbbed through the snow.

When we got home I rushed into the house. Mother, when she followed, having paid Jack, had lost her happy mood. "Twenty pounds!" she snorted. "That Campbell robber charged me twenty pounds."

Twenty pounds was a huge sum – more than a week's wages. Campbell's taxi was blackballed for us for all time. When he got himself a coach and we sometimes had no alternative but to use it my Mother would fume. "That robber!" Years and years later she still flinched at even the mention of his name and would mutter "Robber!" under her breath.

I did not rest for long on my Scarlet Fever laurels. My next effort was a cough – not just a cough but a cough, cough, cough all day every day. The doctor came and listened to me and was obviously impressed.

The minister came and that really was a sign that things were serious. Peter told me that they thought I had T.B. I did not know what T.B. was but it was obviously enough to get the big players moving.

Mr MacDougall gave me a book and I took it "thank you". "No, no, I want you to touch my hand," he said and took my hand in his.

I had learned enough in church and Sunday School to know that the hands of Jesus had power but I was surprised and not unimpressed to find that the minister seemed to think that he might share the gift. But there was no electric shock or rush of power, his hand was soft and cool and I just carried on coughing.

He said a prayer, pausing when my coughs threatened to drown out his line to God.

This time there was no ambulance. We cycled down to Ardgay and mother and I got the bus to Golspie to see some specialist who came up there for a day from Inverness.

He listened to my cough and my chest and peered down my throat and told us that it was a 'relaxed throat'. They would keep me in the hospital to treat it but it was, he assured my mother, no great worry.

Mother went off home alone on the bus and I was led into the ward in which I had a few years earlier been unwelcome as a visitor. It must have been a sad day for the group of quiet men who resided there when I was ensconced in the corner and proceeded to bark at them.

On the morning of the day, a week later, when the wee specialist man from Inverness came back I awoke and did not cough.

The men looked at me as if I was a stranger: "who the hell are you?" their eyes asked.

The wee man was delighted and took full credit for my recovery. I did wonder if maybe God and MacDougall had had a hand in it but I kept that to myself.

No taxi home this time. Bus to Ardgay where my bike awaited my return and the next Monday I was back to school.

I was not finished yet. I had another trick up my sleeve and it was a good one. It gave me weeks off school, complete freedom to wander round the farm and until Doctor Lindsay got to work, no pain.

What I got was ringworm. Boys on farms and crofts were forever picking up ringworm from the cattle and it was a simple matter to be rid of it and back to school in a week. I am unsure why my little drama turned into such a performance. It could be that I got it on my face and it could be that Dr Lindsay had a series of off days. Dr Lindsay was a lady of skeletal build, who smoked heavily and coughed dramatically. When overtake by a fit of coughing she would gradually slide down behind her desk to reappear with watering eyes and heaving for breath. My mother would say, "It's a shame bothering the poor woman – she's far more ill than we are." But Doctor Lindsay proved her wrong – she lived with her fags and her coughs into her late eighties.

In the case of my ringworm she started gently. It spread from ear to ear, round my chin and down my neck and was like a full beard without the moustache. Doctor Lindsay's first effort was a vivid purple lotion, which gave my beard a spectacular appearance but did nothing to lessen the problem. We moved from purple to a green potion which, when mottled with the purple, made me look like a buddleia bush. But again no improvement was evident.

Doctor Lindsay's great asset was her persistence. When the purple and green had been given time and had proved useless she moved on to iodine.

Up to then my sickness had been very relaxing, no school, no pain, and no problem.

When we moved to iodine the course was steeply down hill. The iodine hurt. Dr. Lindsay's method of application was a piece of cotton wool in forceps, dipped in the iodine and vigorously rubbed in. She had, seemingly, at the same time a shortage of cotton wool so the tiny piece she dipped each time very swiftly disappeared and it felt as if she was rubbing with just the sharp end of the forceps.

Now my beard was even bigger – it had swollen considerably so that my chin was lost – and now it was a dingy, dark brown. Mother had reached breaking point and went to see Doctor Lindsay. What was said at that meeting I was never made privy to but the outcome was that I was sent to Raigmore Hospital.

Again no ambulance but me and mother on the bikes to Ardgay and then an unprecedented ride on the bus to Inverness with my brown beard attracting a lot of attention.

The man in Inverness poked my beard with a dubious finger and tutted. I was whisked off by a nurse and she stuck a syringe in my bum. I was returned to Mother and we retraced our long journey home.

Next day the swelling had gone down. The day after my chin reappeared and the brown beard began to flake off. Within a week it was all gone.

As the scarlet fever had left me with a souvenir nose, the ringworm's gift to the future was not evident until I started to shave when, especially with a new blade, I got a lot more bloody mess than most men would expect.

In all the time that I had run my way through these illnesses my siblings had moved smoothly forward without any adventures – I cannot recall them even visiting the doctor.

I packed it in then – I think it was the iodine that did it – and abandoned my invalid career.

The next big disaster did not involve the children – it involved Mother.

HARVEST

I tried to divert attention and spread the meaning of Harvest by rambling on about harvests of turnips, potatoes, hay and even sheep. But no one is fooled. There is but one Harvest in all our minds – the Harvest that brings forth thanks giving services, when the church is decked out in fruit and veg. That, too, is an effort to widen the meaning of 'harvest' – always in the church display are potatoes and turnips, cabbages and carrots, cauliflowers and marrows but not, thankfully, sheep. Central though are the sheaves of corn – wheat, barley and oats.

The main cereals in our neck of the woods were oats and barley; the latter aimed at the whisky business for they paid a premium.

Fields were planted and sown right up to the boundary fences so before the tractor and the binder were brought in a squad scythed a band all round the field. The loose straw was gathered and tied into sheaves by a band of the self same straw and they were leaned against the fence to dry.

When the tractor pulled the binder into the field and started its circuit of cutting, we followed behind bowing like worshippers stooking the sheaves. The devil for the stokers was in the thistles. For the men it was the knotter in the binder. There would be regular hold-ups when the followers realised that the sheaves, which the binder spat out, were not tied. The tractor would be yelled to a halt and the men would gather round the knotter to inspect and curse and cajole. For the men it was a puzzle when the mechanism went wrong. For me it was a wonderment - which lasts still - that any machine could tie a knot so my puzzlement was when it went right.

As the standing oats retreated to the middle of the field the boys and the dogs got excited. Suddenly there would be a fireworks display as jumping jack rabbits broke from cover to be tossed by dogs and rugby tackled by lumbering boys. It was a harvest bonus, which produced rabbit stews in the succeeding days.

If the weather was good the reaping went on into the dusk and such days lay an impression of beauty on my mind, which is still as fresh as it was more than fifty years ago.

The binder sails turning, white and unhurried, in the gloom the pale gleam of the corn and above it all the moon - huge, low and silver.

Like when haymaking the worriers had a permanent eye on the sky. There were dangers to the crop in too much rain but I was never aware that it was as much as a threat as it was to the hay. I recall one year when a high tide and a high river combined to flood the bottom end of a field of stooks and the floating sheaves were lost, but they were only a few. There was in the shape of the sheaves and the stooks a steep, shiny surface, which rapidly drained the rain away.

Of the two cereals oats was much the favourite. It was a simple head of grass like seeds whereas barley heads were prettily feathered with brush like yavings. Yavings broke off the seeds and got into clothes and, like little hacksaw blades; they were armed with itchy teeth that also made them mobile. They were a curse and got everywhere – in boots, in pants, in hair – there was no place too private for their exploration.

Again we boys were the load builders when school did not get in the way. We would have preferred to be on the tractor but that cushy job was given to one of the old fellows like Gordon or Watt. There was a skill to building a load of sheaves as there was to building a stack but both were more ordered and more secure than the hay harvest.

To build a good load on a trailer the sheaves were lined along the sides first, grain end inwards, and the middle filled only later. This allowed the sheaves to slope slightly into the load – they were slippery so were always insecure. The trip to the stack yard was a swaying test and there was never a year when at least one of the loads slipped off – as we, the builders, were on top we jumped clear but we had no one to blame but ourselves, though we sometimes accused Watt of speeding!

The stack building was little short of an art and the final results were scrutinised and criticised from every angle. But a stack yard full of rows of beautiful, matching stacks was a joy. All the local farmers and workers would slow to pass another's stack yard and smile if they saw a soldier out of line.

Like building the load in the field the job of building the stack got harder as it got taller. To start by forking the sheaves off a high load down onto a stack base was simple but as the stack grew and the loads reached the floor it got harder and harder.

Again it was a time for all hands on deck. My father was one who went down to the stack yard in the evening after work and gave a hand. He had not timed it well, a stack was nearly done and he got the job of forking the sheaves up. He got home and collapsed into his chair with pain in muscles he did not know that he had – but he was back next night and luckier for a new stack was just starting.

Gradually the stack yard filled and the fields emptied. They looked sad and bare with dull stubble and only livened when the flocks of geese cruised in, with a great chorus of cries and announced that winter was on its way.

GUISING

Towards the end of October the children of Invercarron began to take an unusually keen interest in turnips. In the turnip shed figures were to be seen clambering over the great pile of roots – lifting, scanning, rejecting and finally dubiously selecting one, taking it to the door to study it closely in the daylight. Not only must the selected turnip be large it must be the right shape – and for once it did not matter if it was a yellow or a swede.

The work of hollowing out the turnip was time consuming unless, like me, you had a brother who was a too old to go guising but who could be prevailed upon to demonstrate how the job should be done. For hollowing some used a knife but our family favourite was a sharp-sided spoon that lay at the back of the scullery drawer from one year to the next until called on in this moment of need.

It was a requirement to hollow the turnip to as near the skin as could be risked without breaking through. The eyes and nose holes were always triangular. It was the mouth which allowed for personal preference and individual flair. It was important to make the initial mouth opening little more than a narrow slit for that allowed the cutting away of irregular sections to leave fangs and jagged teeth.

When the candle inside was lit and the artwork viewed in the dark the more grotesque the mouth the better we were pleased. The grotesqueness of the face was soon matched by the nastiness of the smell as the heat of the candle got to work on the turnip's innards –"Get that stinking thing out to the shed!" – Mother would yell as the smell spread from the scullery into the living room.

The other big and time-consuming preparation was the manufacture of a false face. There was a search for cereal boxes, cornflakes were considered best –big and the card was not too stiff. It must reach right across the face from ear to ear and from high on the brow to below the chin. This was essential to stop nosy old biddies from peering in at an angle and solving our identity.

One of the refinements on the face once the nose, eyes and mouth had been cut out and the application of as much colour as we could manage was the addition pf a border of sheep's wool glued on to represent a fine big beard and side burns. Hamish one year attached a beard of finely cut strips of newspaper and we were all immensely impressed by this innovation and the next year everyone in our group, except Hamish, had newspaper beards. Sadly it rained, the newsprint ran and the paper turned to pulp. It was a fashion statement that did not reappear.

Clothes were easy. In our shed my father had a chest of drawers full of clothes – including lots of ladies dresses. Before you get the wrong idea let me assure you that this collection of clothes, which he hoarded, was for use as winter insulation in his beehives. There was a share out of the garb between the guisers. These extras added to old army tunics and coats gave us each a satisfactory variation. The common head gear were bonnets and these could be trimmed at the back with a bit of fleece to cover the back of the wearers head – this was necessary to disguise the long hair of the girls – all be it tied up – from the short back and sides of the boys.

As you will have gathered we laid great importance on making our disguises total. We reckoned it a failure if someone in one of the houses we visited recognised us. But in reality the local houses expected only the local children so one did not have to be a wizard to guess who was who. But still we persisted and a lot of the folk we visited played along with the mystery.

To add to the sartorial disguise we adopted strange voices. The boys all spoke in high squeaks, which we felt sure echoed, a girly tone and the girls all tried to speak down in their boots and sounded like excited old men.

As soon as it was dark on Hallowe'en we joined up and set off. The first houses we visited were our own and then the nearest, like Gordons and Thains, and then we returned the youngest of our group to home and started out in earnest.

The candles in the turnips invariably blew out and even when lit gave no light but plenty of stink. Householders told us severely "Don't take that in here!" and when the one box of matches we possessed ran out we abandoned the turnip lanterns, some just left on a doorstep and some we tossed into the ditch and depended on our battery flash lights from our bikes.

Our receptions varied drastically.

At Gordon's we were asked in and while the old man looked on quietly his Missus would circle each of us like a cobra peering and poking. "Soft hands," she peered at my hands." A girl for sure." My companions all sniggered but Mrs G. did not notice.

We were given an apple and two barley sugar sweets each.

At Bratchie's we were not even invited in. He answered the door and we could see her peeping round the kitchen door. He shut the door when he went back in and came back and handed an apple to each of us – tasty enough little ones which came from the garden, we had sampled them earlier in the year on a clandestine visit.

On the year that the Sweets were in residence at Hallowe'en we knocked on the door. Samantha opened up about half an inch, saw a group of short ghouls, gave a little scream and slammed the door. "Daft bitch", someone said. "We would have been OK if he had been home," I said, feeling defensive on the Sweets behalf.

Our visit to the Big House was strange. The MacNamaras obviously were unaware of what was expected of them at Hallowe'en by the guising fraternity. We would knock on the big front door and listen to the chorus of dog threats from within. This was followed by the current maid shouting and doors slamming. Finally the maid, who we knew was one of the Ross lassies from Strathcarron and was only a few years older than us, opened the door.

"They're at their dinner," she shrugged as if recognising that it was a ridiculous time to be eating. "Wait though, I'll go and see."

We were left in the giant hallway, peering at the staircase and walls of deep, dark wood, the floor too was shining wood and scattered with great big skin rugs with fanged heads smiling at us.

"Here," the Ross lassie returned and handed over a pound note. "Share that between you."

It was not disappointing. Last year we had got half-a-crown each and this worked out at four bob each – it more than covered inflation.

It was a long hike to the next couple of houses, one at the sawmill and one at the cross roads beside the bridge. It would have been easy to carry on up to Corvost, to Kenny the Tailor's or over the bridge to the keepers and to Oaklea but that would be overstepping our boundary – these places were not in our territory. Instead it was the long walk back and up towards Culrain and Watt's and Matheson's and even Angie's.

In each house we performed much the same repertoire. Hamish had a poem about a magpie – a bird that did not choose to live with us but we forgave it. Betty had a joke about a frog and a princess in which the kiss resulted in the princess changing into a frog. She did not tell it very well and it was not funny the first time we heard it and was deeply unfunny on the tenth rendition.

Hamish and I did a double talk thing like we heard on the radio. "I say, I say, I say, my dog's got no nose." "How does he smell?" "Awful." Most folks had heard it on the radio but had the civility to smile – there was, after all, the bonus of it being a 'live' show.

To round off we all joined together and gave a rousing rendition of "I belong to Glasgow". It was a tune we all knew and it mattered not that none of us had ever been near Glasgow.

While we younger ones were finishing off our guising round and tallying our money and counting apples and sweets more sinister groups were preparing to swing into action.

For this one night of the year the older boys and young men were afflicted with a kind of madness, which the older generation, who had been inflicted with the same virus in their youth, for the most part condoned.

Staid steady people like my parents and Old Duncan would laugh and applaud the most outrageous vandalism which on any other date would have them tutting and snorting.

There was the run of the mill stuff which was predictable and boring – gates removed and hidden, carts and trailers swapped around between crofts and farms and horse moved – a crofter would find in the morning that he had a chestnut instead of a grey and at the same time a neighbour along the strath would find that his chestnut had gone grey overnight.

Some crofters and householders went to extreme lengths to safeguard themselves. Gates were chained and pad locked, carts and farm machines were chained together. Those who saw these precautions shook their heads – if ever one wished to attract action the surest way was to try to make it impossible. The same applied to the idiots who made a big fuss about some misdemeanour last year. The ones who smiled or chuckled at the attention they had received were the ones with the least to worry about this year.

Word flew about the next day and, on his route, Father was perfectly placed to pick up every detail.

Jackie Ross had chained his cart to a heavy plough; the plough had been lifted into the cart and trundled off to the centre of a neighbour's field. Col Ross, Jackie's neighbour, had chained and padlocked his front gate to the retaining strainer post. In the night the strainer was dug up and it and the gate, still securely chained, went off to Jackie's steading and roosted on the roof of the byre.

Old Rob Bain was a well-known complainer about what he termed 'The Hallowe'en Thugs'. He had a wee Austin A40 and it was bodily lifted and parked sideways across his door with nose and tail no more than six inches from walls. He had to use a tractor with a hoist and a full vocabulary of bad language to get it out.

To damage anything was frowned on. If a gate was broken or thrown into the river or a pond it was looked on as not playing the game.

Tommy Gray was an old fellow wise in the way of Hallowe'en. He had two gates and he simply removed them and locked them in his shed. Secure and satisfied he and Molly sat by the fire and the rascals silently scaled his roof and put a turf on his chimney. With streaming eyes and words unsuitable in a church elder's mouth Tommy raged out into the night and set off to borrow his son and his ladder.

There was no one immune from this attention.

At the school, while Mr Smith was in stern control, his wheelbarrow was taken from his garden and parked on top of the newly erected cast iron bicycle shed. It was not a remarkably daring, clever or amusing act but we pupils were all delighted – not because of the act but because of the victim.

The Church of Scotland manse was a very smart house with a gravel drive on which Mr MacDougall parked his Ford Popular. In front of his door was a raised flag stone area with little pillared stonewalls on each side and three stone steps all along the front. He did have a garage in which the car normally slept but on one Hallowe'en he either forgot to put it away or thought that he and his car were protected by divine providence. It was no surprise to any one except Mr and Mrs MacDougall when in the morning they found the car parked on the front patio. Mr MacDougall had to go cap in hand to the football team coach and borrow the team to lift his car back down – there is no doubt that some of those lifting it down had been involved in lifting it up.

It was Ken the Bobby's custom to keep a low profile at all times and at Hallowe'en he went so low as to be invisible. What could the poor man achieve? And calling on him guaranteed the complainant special attention next year. But, of course, some folk did not know that. The Sidneys were new to the place – returned from tea planting somewhere – and when they spotted dark figures heading off up Ardgay Hill with their fancy wrought iron gate they rang the constabulary.

Then, unlike now, the local bobby did not have the luxury of pleasing himself if he answered a call for help – he knew it was a waste of time but he also knew the type of people the Sidneys were and he got out his bike and pedaled majestically down to the scene of the crime.

There was a lot of shoulder shrugging on Ken's part in the ensuing interview and a lot of 'buts' and 'goodness gracious' on the Sidneys side when Ken tried to explain the communal madness, which was Hallowe'en.

Poor Ken came out of the Sidneys well aware that he had not succeeded in conveying to them that their gate would turn up next day unharmed. He had to walk home – he was not surprised to find that during his time in the Sidney's his bike had gone. It was found next day hanging on the 'Police' sign at the corner of his house. Ken had the good sense to laugh it off and call the terrorists 'rascals'.

The Sidneys got their gate back for a year and the following year both their front and back gates disappeared – the latter never found – and their front and back doors were tied so that they would not open and Mr Sidney had to make an undignified exit from the window. They did not consult the police on this occasion and tried to smile about it – they were rewarded by being crossed off the most wanted list.

There is no doubt that there were those who overstepped the parameters of what was acceptable. Scores were settled under the cover of Hallowe'en pranks. Tractors were pushed into rivers and lochs, machinery disappeared and there were cases where the missing articles turned up in use miles away. Some activity left damage, one croft house had all its windows painted black and no amount of scraping could remove it all – the glass had to be replaced.

Gradually the excesses of the few brought the whole tradition into disrepute and what had been regarded as trickery was moved into the column headed 'Vandalism' in the Police records. And the police were different – they came in from town in cars and their sympathies lay with the people like themselves, town raised and jealous of their property.

Who is to say that it is a bad thing that on the first of November carts are not teetering on barn roofs and turf sods do not top unsuspecting chimney pots?

JUNO

There were dogs, of course. Every crofter and farmer had a barking bonanza of collies. There were working dogs everywhere. But pet dogs were not thick on the ground. Perhaps so soon after the war there was a more pressing need.

There were, of course, the Admiral's two black labs "Scapa" and "Flow" who you will recall were responsible for the swift acceleration of the Invercarron children. Lady Mac had an ancient spaniel that ambled along in the lady's brisk wake.

Hamish and I had a close encounter with that old dog – we were spending an evening sampling the apple crop in the Big House garden, I was up one tree, Hamish was in the one alongside, when suddenly he hissed at me and pointed down and I was alarmed to find the old dog sniffing round the base of my tree and cocking her head to look up at me. We became aware of Lady M's sharp American voice and the deep rumble of Gardner Bratchie's response. They were just yards away and we felt very exposed – the trees were small and we were no more than six feet off the ground and they had just to turn their heads to see us, they only had to wonder what that old fool spaniel was looking up at. Thankfully for us they took no notice of the dog and she decided she better keep ambling along or she would be left behind.

Watt had a pet dog. It was reputed to be a Jack Russell terrier but it was a bit short on the leg and long on the ear –"There's a bit of Spaniel in there somewhere," Watt would admit. Watt's mode of transport was an ancient motorbike and an open sidecar. His dog who was named "Muffin" – "stupid bloody name" Watt said and blamed it on his sister – stood in the sidecar facing the breeze – she was never in danger, Watt did not go fast, we could overtake him on our bikes every time. But, yes, there was one accident. Willie Matheson's mother regularly boxed up a box of eggs and sent them to some relative in Edinburgh. Willie was belting along to the Post Office in Culrain with the egg box when, on the Z-bend under the railway he met Watt. Watt was going gently but Willie was not. He shot off the bike and landed on the verge, and Muffin, who with surprising agility had taken cover in the body of the side-car, jumped back up to her perch and yapped angrily. "My eggs, my eggs!" Willie wailed. "Shut up you damn fool!" Watt addressed Muffin sternly and she took no notice and then turned his attention to Willie. He studied him gingerly and then bent and pulled him up "Get up you daft bugger, there's nothing wrong with your legs."

Old Duncan had an old mat of a sheepdog called "Scotty" who was old, grey and short legged but he turned into a tornado when he spotted rats.

On a whim Old Duncan got himself a wee Shetland collie. He called it "Boddach" and it was a very pretty little thing with black, gold and white and a sharp foxy nose. When Old Duncan drove his Baby Austin Boddach stood on a cushion on the front seat and looked out. She yapped if a bird flew by or if she saw another dog. Old Duncan was mortified when he moved the car one day, heard a yelp and felt a bump. Boddach had been lying in the shade by the front wheel. "It was a yappy little bugger," Watt said, "But not a nice way to go."

One shepherd called his dog "Hoy" – he would never admit if it was so called to flatter MacNamara and match his Scapa and Flow, or if it was just laziness that prompted him.

These were dogs whose names stood out as being exotic and unusual. On every side there were "Glens", "Bobs", "Nells", "Mosses" and so on. When we got a dog she would have what we judged to be a very posh name – embarrassingly posh I thought – she was called "Juno".

Jean was in her first job working for some couple in Bonar. Her duties were to look after a couple of children. As a sideline these people bred dogs. Juno was a beautiful golden retriever, but she was a tramp and a hussy and fell for a non-pedigree interloper - and as a result received a death sentence.

Jean came home with the tearful news and it was unanimously agreed that pregnant Juno could not die and so she came to us.

The pups when born bore out her lack of taste in the matter of lovers for they were brown and black. Father gave them away – well, that is what he told me and I was glad to accept that as the truth.

The wood shed was altered and a big, comfy box was built in to fit Juno. She was well provided with straw and she lived a life of luxury.

Jean was courting a policeman about this time. He came to visit one day and we were all out except for Juno. With swishing tail she let him in to sit by the fire and only took exception when he decided to get out of the chair to go to the toilet. She snarled and growled and told him in no uncertain terms to stay in the chair.

We got home in the dusk a few hours later to find the beau sitting in the dark beside a dead fire with everything crossed.

We laughed and teased and could not believe that Juno would put the mockers on anyone. She was a big softy. She could carry sea gull eggs in her mouth without breaking them. She sometimes, much to her own surprise, caught a rabbit but she was totally incapable of killing it.

She was at times an embarrassment. I remember a summer evening when everyone in Invercarron was out and about and Juno fled across to the steading and met with that sly old devil Matt. It took just a moment for them to agree that at that moment sex would be good and having very publicly performed their union found that when it was time to part they could not. Most of the watchers laughed but none of my family did – we were ashamed of our beautiful girl. She was treated with reserve for several days after that.

She was not overly obedient. When we went out for a walk and Father was in tow she was as good as gold – he had only to shout and she would abandon her rabbit chase and come lolloping up smiling.

When, however, she had a young pretender such as me to answer to she felt no inclination to obey. Many times I chased across fields and hill shouting and whistling and practically weeping with temper but Juno did not come until she was ready and then she circled and sniggered.

It was the back end and I had a tattie holiday job lined up on the tractor putting the dung out. Invercarron was not a big grower of spuds so I was delighted to get the much sought after job of driving the tractor and trailer of dung slowly down the fields while the dung was unloaded into spaced heaps.

Then Mother got ill. It was unknown territory. That she could not get out of bed seemed bizarre and the whole thing puzzled me more than it worried me.

By this time I was the last child at home. Jean was married and away in Melvich, Barbara was working in the Co-op in distant Langholm and Peter was in the Royal Navy. There was never any question of Father taking time off work – jobs were scarce and not to be risked. So it fell to me to stay home and be day nurse but I was a totally selfish child and had looked forward to my holiday job and was not going to give it up without a fight. It was Mother who had the final say and she said, "Let him go. What's he going to do stuck in the house with me?"

So guiltily I went to drive the Fergie in the chill stubble fields and raced home at dinnertime and let Juno out and gave Mother tea.

After work I got the dinner going with instructions from the sick bed. Mother could not eat but she insisted that Father and I must.

Jeannie came a couple of times, just for the day, she had to get back for Auntie Annie.

Old Mrs Gordon came over to visit one day while Jeannie was there. It was the furthest any of us had seen her move – fully a hundred yards across the little park.

It was not a successful visit. I never did know what took place but Jeannie took an instant dislike (Jeannie could weigh a character and come to an unerring conclusion in less than fourteen seconds.) "Dreadful woman," she said. "Mad as a hatter."

Even Mother was unimpressed by the visit. "A queer soul yon – What poor old Gordon must have to put up with!"

Jean came too but only for a day or two. "She has her own to look after now, " Mother said.

Then, thankfully, the doctor saw sense, an ambulance came and Mother was whisked away to Inverness where in Raigmore Hospital they detected a brain tumour and rushed her off to Aberdeen where so delicate a problem could be treated.

For Father, Juno and me it was a time of emptiness. We were not just a ship without a sail; we were missing the captain and crew as well.

Father was up first and let Juno out and when he had gone to work I had what was left of the porridge and shut Juno in when I went off to school.

Luckily, Father was on our run so he was back on his round about midday and gave Juno a run and I was home around four. But it was not enough. Juno welcomed us and swished her tail but she was always looking past us. When I opened a room door she pushed frantically past to look but she was always disappointed and looked at me with puzzled sad eyes. "No, she's no there – but she'll be home soon." I would say but Juno would just throw herself down on the mat in front of the fire and lay her nose on her paws and pine.

Meanwhile, we wrote letters to Aberdeen and sometimes Father rang from the phone box in Ardgay. In my letters I tried to be cheery and told her what I had cooked and what I had done at school and always ended by saying how we missed her, me, Daddy and Juno.

I was in charge of the catering - a case of giving the job to the only available recruit. I had dinner in school but I cooked a meal every evening. I did straightforward things like mince or sausages and tatties, or chops and tatties. Or more adventurous things like a bacon and egg flan in short crust pastry to die for. And one day a kind of shepherd's pie but between the tatties and the mince I inserted a layer of mashed turnip – it was good.

Folk still gave my father presents on his rounds but they changed in one detail. Now the salmon was already cooked, the hen already roasted and on a couple of occasions he came home carefully bearing casseroles of stewed venison – enough to do us for two or three days.

But none of that cheered us and Juno wilted and faded and would not eat. Father left a message for the vet to call when he was next in Invercarron – a dog did not rate high in the vetinerary list and did not merit a separate special visit. A cow or a horse was worth money so they came at the top of the ranking.

But Juno did not wait. Father and I went out to see her in the morning and she was stiff and dead. That night by the light of a lantern he dug a grave between two trees and we wrapped Juno in a khaki great coat and laid her in the earth.

I wept buckets and will remember that chill dark evening forever.

But in the morning when I went to the school bus I laughed when I told Willie Matheson that Juno was dead. Why did I do that? What a traitor!

There was a note through the door a few days later,

'Called but no sign of a dog', signed Vet.

I still wrote my letters but did not mention Juno – Father thought it best to leave such sad news. So I wrote about school and cooking but signed off just Daddy and me. I could obey by not mentioning Juno but I could not lie and send mother the dead dog's love.

At last Mother got the nod that she could go home. It was a long trip so father arranged that she spend a few days with his brother Davey and his wife Rosie who lived in Aberdeenshire. On Saturday they would bring Mother home and then go on to Bogan and visit Granny and go home on Sunday.

I spent Saturday making sandwiches and laying out plates of Bowie's pies and sausage rolls and we had a big Swiss roll oozing rasp jam.

Mother arrived at dusk. She looked thinner and older and it seemed like an inner light had faded but she hugged me and we both cried and then Father brought in Davey and Rosie after a suitable pause.

I made the tea and we all sat round the table and they all complimented me on the spread and I thought I would burst with pride and happiness.

When Mother was not looking Rosie mouthed "Dog?" to me but with a shake of the head and a stupid grin I confused her even more.

It was dark when Davey and Rosie left. Mother and I stood in the doorway and waved while Father guided them with a torch to the car. By the time the car was going up the hill and about to from our sight Father gave a final wave with the flashlight – he did not know it then but that was the last time he would see his little brother who would emigrate without a word soon after – and joined us in the doorway.

"So Juno's gone then," Mother said and it was not a question.

We all wept – I think even father – for our love lost and our love returned.

THE CONCERT

The likes of the Howing Match and the Dog Trials each had to raise funds, particularly the Howing match for they did not even charge admission and had a barrow load of prizes to finance, and their fund raisers fell into three main categories. Dances were always popular and got the cash in. Another even bigger money-spinner was a Sale of Work. And finally there was the concert.

Mother was a keen contributor and buyer from the Sales. She would bake cakes and fancies and cart them off and come home with a bag of cakes baked by someone else. We were never convinced that it was a fair swap.

One time she came home with a potted Hydrangea – it had a massive blue flower the size of a football. She was swooning at the beauty of it.

"Old Mrs Gill, the witch, saw me with it, 'Oh' she shouts, 'I was after that. I hope it dies!' Imagine! Right in front of everyone she said it."

None of us were in the least surprised when a few days later the prize plant wilted and died. We were all convinced that the curse of Mrs Gill had done the business, but on reflection it may have been that the poor plant could not stand our room having been raised in the Glasshouse at Gledfield House.

The first port of call by a concert organiser was to the local primary school and rope in every kid with the slightest vestige of talent and sufficient cockiness to perform solo. Those who were left were formed into a choir. That way you every proud parent, all the siblings, and a good percentage of Grannies and Granddads and aunties and uncles, felt duty bound to come and pay to see their off spring perform.

That was what they did when they put on a concert in the old Balnagown Hall in Ardgay and it worked every time.

First, of course, you booked your stars.

A concert would not be worth the name if it did not feature Davy Stag. He was a local postie, po-faced and sober so it was all the more wonderful when he pranced onto the stage in his Harry Lauder guise with a crooked stick, a huge feather in his toorie and a distemper brush for a sporran.

Davy performed songs, which he composed about local issues. Sometimes he ruffled some feathers. His ditty about the church elders ' who made a good week's wage when standing at the plate' did not go down well with the church elders. He had one about Colin Campbell's aeroplane that contained dialogue between a passenger and Colin in which the passenger enquired what those black things were on a distant road. The response was that if they were moving they were crows but if they were stationary they were County roadmen. That did not go a breeze with the roadmen or their wives. But happily for Davy elders and roadmen were heavily outnumbered and we kids and other non-sophisticates cheered him 'till we were hoarse.

In our diet of fiddles and accordions George Peat was a welcome change. When the big man ambled onto the stage he put a shining saxophone to his lips and blew and blew us all away. Such novelty was received with rapturous clapping and foot stamping and then George amazed us even further. He laid aside his sax, took a deep breath and sang. Not a baritone or tenor softie voice but a voice from the depths. We had all heard records of Paul Robeson but we had never seen a real, live man who could produce such a voice. And his songs were about such strange things too, 'Mud' and 'Deep Rivers' among them.

Later we were introduced to a man who had come all the way from Invergordon - a distant place then - so we weren't entirely surprised when he did such an outlandish thing as produce a saw and a bow and proceed to produce magic music full of high, wavering notes the like of which we had never heard before.

The rest of the offerings were left to the kids.

The first offering was the so-called 'choir'. They had been coached by the schoolteacher and she had had enough sense to let them loose on well-worn old favourites which the audience felt obliged to join in. The volume of the audience's contribution was enough to cover the choir's deficiencies.

We had loads of kids who could carry a tune. Some could remember the words. But there was only a handful who could manage both.

Interspersed between the child singers there were musicians and one brave lad who gave a recitation which did not make a lot of sense, I suspected that he got his verses mixed up. He denied it hotly on Monday when I casually mentioned it, and I withdrew the slur when he threatened to punch my head.

A pair of podgy girls played fiddles. Their first rendering was a tune unknown to the audience but we gave them credit for reaching the end at roughly the same time and we roared our approval. Their second effort was their undoing for it was vaguely recognised and their faults were cruelly exposed. The artists may have recognised this for they picked up the pace and raced to the end. It didn't matter - they got a big cheer and left the stage blushing and giggling.

One of my classmates did a turn on the accordion. The instrument was much bigger than he was and the only evidence we could trace that there was indeed a boy behind the accordion was two chubby hands and, above, two darting, scared eyes and a thatch of red hair. He played fast tunes but he played them slowly. That was accepted - we all knew that he was a learner.

One might assume from my uncomplimentary remarks about my fellow performers that I was a star turn. Not quite!

I was a chubby child with a shock of black hair, a tweed jacket, which had fitted perfectly a year before, and a voice like an angel.

We all had two songs ready. There was no question of failing to be asked for an encore - if such had happened we would have trundled out our second rendition anyway. My two songs were 'The Isle of Mull' and a soppy pop of the time called 'The Loveliest night of the Year'. My Mum had said it was a daft song for a wee kid to sing but she had been outgunned by my two elder sisters.

Jessie on the piano was familiar with 'The Isle of Mull' but not the other. "You just start off and I'll pick it up", she said.

I was to sing 'The Isle of Mull' first so the worry about accompaniment could be shelved for a few minutes.

I stepped onto the stage, pale, trembling and on the verge of panic. Jessie played an encouraging introduction to the 'The Isle of Mull' and I took a deep breath and launched into 'The Loveliest Night of the Year'.

Jessie ground to a halt after a few puzzled bars, but I had started so I was going to finish. My big sisters were beside my proud parents; they mouthed the words encouragingly and I ploughed on unaccompanied to the end.

If the audience were puzzled they showed no sign and when the applause had subsided sufficiently I flew into 'The Isle of Mull' with fervour while Jessie, who had been surprised by my sudden start, tried to catch up.

"The Isle of Mull is of Isles the fairest.

"Of ocean's gems 'tis the first and rarest."

I can't remember what I did yesterday, but I can remember every word of those songs more fifty years on.

What joy! What relief! I bowed and grinned, bathed luxuriantly in the clapping and stamping. They loved me and I loved them. I sidled to the side of the stage, ducked round the curtain and went back to my seat meeting on the way a pale-faced, sweating waif carrying a chanter.

Now I was free to enjoy the entertainment. Gone were the butterflies, dried up were the sweaty palms and, under the gaze of the dusty stags' heads, I could whoop and holler with the rest of the crowd.

I looked around me at the known faces and they all smiled and I felt part not only of my family but also of the village – It was a feeling of luxurious comfort and it was the last of that time.

Concerts were being organised by professional entertainers like Calum Kennedy and Andy Stewart and we were shown to be a poor shadow of these. Young folk were leaving – going to National Service, University and for jobs in the cities and not many were coming back.

Farms which had employed a squad of men and housed their families, could manage with one man able to operate the modern machines. The farm cottages were sold off as holiday houses or simply allowed to fall into ruin. Gordon's house had its gable end removed and was used to shelter the combine harvester.